CONTENTS

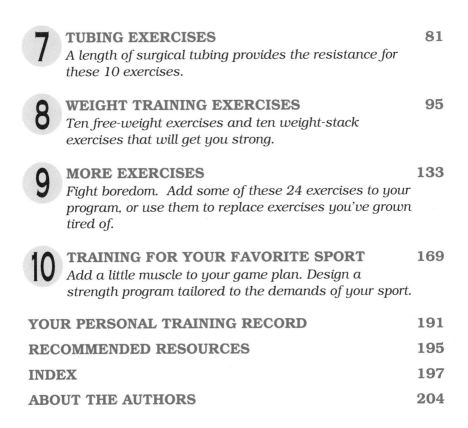

Strength Through Resistance: An Introduction

How to Get Hot Buns. That's the title of a magazine article we came across recently. We'd like to tell you we saw it in a gourmet cooking journal. But it was in a women's fitness magazine, and the buns referred to were of the anatomical variety. This was another miracle workout in the search for the perfect body (or at least one part of the perfect body).

No chrome. No pool. No music. Just iron. So read the slogan on a T-shirt we saw advertising a weightlifters' gym: A catchy phrase, to be sure, and one that certainly confirms who the place is for and what you'll find when you get there.

These are just two examples of the unbalanced and restrictive approaches to strength training that continue to amaze and amuse us. Luckily, there are facilities that have a pool, play some music, and welcome a broad clientele. And the "hot buns" approach? Articles like this reinforce for us the continuing need for reasoned and rational educational information on strength training for people of all ages, abilities, and inclinations. That's what this book is all about.

The Straight Goods. This is the phrase that best describes our book. You'll find no puff, frills, or fillers here. What you *will* find is straightforward, practical information for safe, effective, and enjoyable training routines.

The title tells it all. Follow the advice offered herein and you will know the basics you need to improve and maintain your strength. It's definitely a *sensible* and essential guide to training. Who doesn't want to be healthier, more fit, or more proficient at a favorite sport? *Strength Basic's* brand of *resistance training* can help you do it.

Resistance training? Let's make sure we're clear on this term before anything else is said. The information below should help.

Getting the Words Straight

Strength training is the umbrella term long used in the field. It's simple and it makes sense since strength training is any training activity to develop strength.

Weight training is a term that has been used over the years as well. It's a logical description when weights are used to train for strength improvement.

Resistance training is yet another term in the strength vocabulary. It's a more all-encompassing term and the one we use throughout this book. Resistance training is strength training using some force to resist your body's efforts. The force may or not be a weight—as you'll see when you read on. While the term resistance training is used infrequently, we rely more often on the acronym RT for ease and convenience.

So as you read and use this book, remember:

RT = resistance training

As a sensible guide to RT, this book is organized in a particular manner. Here's an overview of what's included and how best to use it:

- *Chapter 1, Training for Stronger Health*, describes the many benefits of resistance training, offers some tips for different age groups, and highlights some of RT's special applications. By all means, check out the section on benefits; and if you're in a rush to get started, at least read the other sections that apply to you and consider the goal-setting information at the end of the chapter.

Chapters 2, 3, 4, and 5 provide important background information.

■ **Chapter 2, Facts and Fallacies**, notes nine RT fallacies. Each fallacy—*myth*conception, as we like to call it—is followed by the facts of the matter to set things straight. Peruse them all if you like, but read carefully those that might concern you.

■ **Chapter 3, Strong Terms**, covers terminology. This is important, as many of the words and terms introduced here are used regularly throughout the rest of the book.

■ **Chapter 4, Designing Your Program**, provides the mechanics of RT programs and explains why they work that way. You'll appreciate the detail provided here later on if you want to actively tailor your program to your own particular needs and interests, but it deserves at least a quick read before you begin.

■ **Chapter 5, Playing It Safe, Having Fun**, is a must read. It includes an important, pre-exercise questionnaire and helpful information on injury prevention, safety, and motivation. You can use the warm-up routine provided here prior to your training sessions. Be sure to review the *Movin' On* list at the end of the chapter *before* you get into action.

Chapters 6, 7, and 8 include complete routines. At the beginning of each chapter, we are specific as to who the routine is for in terms of age and current activity/fitness levels. Follow these advisories, determine the equipment or facilities you have available, and then choose the appropriate routine.

■ **Chapter 6, Body-Weight Exercises**, provides a series of body-weight exercises—or calisthenics, as they were once known. With no equipment required, this routine can be done in the comfort and convenience of your own home.

■ **Chapter 7, Tubing Exercises**, involves exercises using a length of surgical tubing for resistance. This inexpensive RT "equipment" allows another simple, effective home or travel routine.

- **Chapter 8, Weight Training Exercises**, includes two routines using equipment. One employs free weights, the other stack weights. The format of these routines is the same, and the exercises are very similar. Choose your routine depending on the type of equipment you prefer.

Chapters 9 and 10 go even further.

- **Chapter 9, More Exercises**, provides a catalogue of additional exercises. Any one of the core routines in Chapters 6 to 8 will get you off to a great start, but at some point you'll long for variety. The exercises included here are easily incorporated into your routine by following the simple guidelines we provide.

- **Chapter 10, Training for Your Favorite Sport**, covers sport-specific training. It builds on the information provided throughout the book. For creative types, a sport training chart and a few rules are provided to help you design your own routine. For those who just want to get at it, there are 16 ready-to-use programs for sports, ranging from alpine skiing to wrestling.

Consider the Resistance Training Program Goals form (page 11) before you begin and use Your Personal Training Record (page 194) to help you monitor your progress and stay on track. The Index (beginning on page 197) makes it easy to find your way around the book when you want to locate topics. The Recommended Resources list (page 195) includes our recommendations for those who want more advanced or specific information.

We have both been involved with resistance training for many years. After all this time, we still think there is something very special about it. After an invigorating training session, you feel good; you feel stronger—physically and psychologically. You feel like you can accomplish anything.

We wish you luck with your program, and as you work your way through the material in this book, we urge you to be sensible, be patient, have fun, and get strong!

Brian Cook & Gord Stewart

1

TRAINING FOR STRONGER HEALTH

Welcome to a stronger, healthier life.
We hope that using this book is just one part of what will
become a life-long quest for the many health benefits that
result from a resistance training (RT) program. The benefits of
RT are many, varied—and wonderful.

A properly designed, regular RT program

- improves muscular strength and endurance,
- strengthens the bones,
- helps control blood pressure,
- helps lower LDL ("bad") and raise HDL ("good") cholesterol,

- improves body composition and helps maintain a healthy body weight,

- enhances heart-lung function, and

- contributes to a positive self-image.

In this chapter, we'll detail some of these health benefits and provide special RT tips and advice for different age groups. We'll also look at three special applications of RT, and end with some thoughts about goal-setting.

GOOD FOR THE BODY, GOOD FOR THE MIND

With adequate muscular strength and endurance, you'll accomplish your daily tasks with less fatigue. Your balance and co-ordination will improve, your posture straighten, and your risk of low back pain decrease.

Because it is a weight-bearing activity, RT can offer protection against osteoporosis—a disease in which bones become fragile and weak. (Osteoporosis is a particular risk for older adults, especially women.) During the growing years, RT (and other weight-bearing activities like walking and running) increase the peak bone mineral content attained as the skeleton matures. During the adult years, RT can help delay the age at which bone mineral loss begins and slow the rate of loss when it does occur. Simply stated, the bones will remain stronger longer. For anyone who has observed the debilitating effects of osteoporosis, this is great motivation for a simple RT routine throughout your lifetime.

Positive changes in blood pressure, blood cholesterol, body composition, and heart-lung function resulting from RT *all* contribute to a reduced risk of heart disease. These changes are more readily achieved when programs concentrate on developing muscular endurance and include only short rest intervals between exercises. Maintaining a healthy body weight can also help control non-insulin dependent diabetes.

Then there is the mental side of it. Increased strength, achievement of a healthy body weight, and improvement in other physical activities or sports that result from RT can have a subtle effect on body image, self-esteem, and confidence.

The pursuit of all of these benefits might tempt you to overdo it. This is a good place, then, to emphasize the importance of moderation. Television, magazines, and all sorts of advertising present us with a constant barrage of images of muscular young men and slim young women. This sets up unrealistic expectations for some people, which can lead to inappropriate exercising, unhealthy dieting, and even the use of drugs. The unfortunate use of drugs as a way to enhance the benefits of an RT routine—and the devastating effects they can have—is the focus of the discussion below.

Drugs? Don't Do Them!

We like to live by the following advice: "If you can't say something nice, don't say anything at all." In this case, we'll make an exception.

Any drug use to enhance strength, physique, or performance is *drug abuse*. We hear all too often of amphetamines and anabolic steroids—sometimes called sports drugs—being used by professional and elite amateur athletes. Sadly, their use is increasingly common among college and high school athletes and even nonathletes. Such drug use has no place in sport, where fair play should be valued, or in a healthy lifestyle.

Talk about long-term pain for short-term gain! Inappropriate use of steroids by males can cause breast and prostate enlargement, atrophy (shrinking) of the testicles, reduced sperm count, and impotence. Women using steroids can look forward to increased facial hair, reduced breast size, male pattern baldness, menstrual irregularities, and a deepening voice. In women and men, steroid use can bring on tremors, acne, and hepatitis and increase the risk of heart disease and liver cancer.

Parents and coaches should be on guard. If you suspect anyone you know is using sports drugs, explore the problem immediately. Medical attention may be necessary.

TRAINING THROUGH THE LIFESPAN

RT can play an important and meaningful role in your activities whatever your age. There are some age-specific factors to consider, however. Here are our observations and suggestions.

TRAINING TIPS FOR CHILDREN AND YOUTH

Anyone concerned that RT may be too demanding for children need merely observe a day in the life of an active child to have their fears allayed. The forces experienced by a child during downhill running, for example, are several times body weight and far more than would ever be placed on the body in even the most demanding RT program.

While it is true that young tissue may be more susceptible to injury, this is balanced by the fact that, up until puberty, children have proportionally larger weight-bearing surfaces (hands, knees, elbows, feet, etc.). Children, in fact, seem to be more resilient and less prone to injury during activity than adults. This does not mean, however, that they are free to pursue RT with reckless abandon.

Here are a few suggestions for their programs:

- **Take time to learn.** Proper technique is crucial for injury prevention. Movements should also be controlled, with no bouncing or jerking actions.

- **Ease into it.** Start with body-weight exercises (as in Chapter 6) or the tubing routine (in Chapter 7). They can move on to the routines in Chapter 8 after a good start-up period.

- **Emphasize the development of muscular endurance.** Children should do relatively high repetitions using light resistance, avoiding heavy loads or maximum, all-out efforts.

■ **Shop around for a facility.** Ask for suggestions from a fitness professional or a neighbor or friend who participates. Do a few sessions on a trial or drop-in basis before committing to any sort of term payment or membership. Look for women- or beginner-only time slots and classes that give you the "break-in" period you need to train with confidence.

■ **Do it as you like it.** Train with a partner and use the facility at quiet times at first. Both of these can help you feel more at home.

TRAINING TIPS FOR OLDER ADULTS

In the past, we tended to accept a gradual physical decline as a natural part of aging. But we now know from research that much of this decline is due not to aging itself but to an inactive way of life. Research is also showing that older adults can expect wonderful benefits from a regular RT routine.

We highlighted these benefits at the beginning of the chapter. RT can improve and maintain muscle strength and help keep bones dense and strong. This, in turn, helps reduce the risk of falling and the severity of injury if a fall does occur. This can be a boon for older adults, because falls are a major contributor to reduced mobility and loss of independence.

It's a real pleasure for us when we visit (or train at) different facilities to see so many older adults—of varying abilities—pursuing RT routines. When we advise older adults on their programs, we usually have to remind them that they're not different from most of the other people they see working out; they're just a little older. That means they have to be just a little more sensible and cautious as they progress.

In addition to the advice provided throughout the book, here are a few reminders for older adults—*not* unlike those offered in the two previous sections for younger RT enthusiasts.

■ **Start slowly.** Launch your program with the routine in Chapter 6 or the one in Chapter 7. Move to Chapter 8 later if you like.

- **Read it and heed it.** Use the illustrations and descriptions to learn the proper technique for each exercise you do. Good technique gives you a firm foundation on which to build your program.

- **Be selective.** If you'll be training at some facility, use the *Training Tips for Grown Ups* provided earlier in this chapter to guide you in your choice.

- **If you don't know, ask.** If you're having trouble with an exercise (or any aspect of your routine), seek help from a fitness professional.

- **When in doubt, leave it out.** If an exercise feels uncomfortable or wrong, exclude it from your routine for now. You can replace it with a comparable exercise or go with a shorter program.

- **Make haste slowly.** Later chapters in the book suggest how long to do a certain routine before moving on to a more advanced one, but don't rush. If you want to stick with something for a longer period, do so. You'll get to know what's best for you.

TRAINING FOR SPECIFIC NEEDS

RT can be designed to meet specific needs you may have. Some comments on three of them follow. We don't pretend to provide all the necessary details. Depending on your own situation, you may want to seek—or you may be provided with—direction for a specialized RT program from an appropriate health professional.

FIT FOR WORK

Physically demanding jobs can lead to fatigue and they certainly subject the body to risk of injury. An appropriate RT program provides conditioning that lessens fatigue and adds strength and muscular endurance, thus reducing injury risk.

In Chapter 10, we provide guidelines for creating RT programs for specific sports. The same basic process can be followed to design a fit-for-work routine—whatever your work may be. If you analyze the demands of your job, you can design a program that strengthens the muscles most used, the opposing muscles, and the assisting muscles and stabilizers. You'll also have to decide on your program goals. Should you emphasize strength, power, or muscular endurance? When you know this, you can apply the program variables as described in Chapter 4.

Your strength and overall fitness, proper body mechanics, and a suitable set-up of your work environment help you work more efficiently with less risk of injury. This, in turn, translates into increased job performance. (Strength in the trunk region—the abdominals and the muscles in the back—is particularly important for any lifting or carrying you must do.)

Seek help from a fitness professional, a kinesiologist, or an ergonomist (a workplace-design specialist) if you'd like more fit-for-work advice.

RT AND REHABILITATION

Many people are introduced to RT after an injury or accident, when it is used as a part of their rehabilitation program. Physical and occupational therapists are the health specialists who help assess rehab needs and design individualized programs.

Here is some very simple advice for injury rehabilitation: Listen carefully and do what you're told! Some people don't progress and recover as they should because they don't stick to the program their therapist designs for them. Other people try for too much too soon. They overdo it and have setbacks or injure themselves again. (This is a time when unbounded enthusiasm *doesn't* pay off.)

If you are currently under medical care for a muscle or joint problem, do only the exercises you have been instructed to perform. Your health professional can help you decide when you're ready for the more general routines described in this book.

SPECIAL CHALLENGES

All sorts of individuals face special challenges that affect their ability to be active. Individuals with a physical disability, for example, stand to benefit from RT in some very important ways.

Increased strength can make everyday tasks easier. It also improves posture which can help reduce the aches and pains that accompany long periods of sitting. RT and other physical activities can improve circulation which, in turn, reduces the possibility of blood-pooling and swelling in the legs. And if RT helps maintain a healthy weight, individuals who use wheelchairs (or other mobility aids) to transfer and get around will be able to do so with less effort, making them more mobile.

Special challenges call for special advice. With proper guidance from a health professional, a personalized program can be designed to suit the needs of any individual.

Another special use for RT is training for various sports. This is a popular application of RT, likely be of interest to many readers; for this reason, we cover it in greater detail in Chapter 10.

GOAL SETTING

Research and practical experience show the value of setting goals before launching into any kind of fitness program—RT included. We'd be remiss, then, if we went any further without touching on this important topic.

As we mentioned at the beginning of the chapter, improved health, fitness, and sport performance await those who pursue a sensible and consistent training routine. But you may have some specific things you'd like to accomplish. You might want to improve your upper body strength, for example, or lose a little weight, or overcome pains in your back. If so, use the RT Program Goals form at the end of the chapter to guide you in your goal-setting efforts. Consider the following as you do it:

- Make your goals specific.

- Be realistic and sensible.

- Write down your goals.

- Use the goals you set as a guide once you get beyond the start-up period and you take a more active part in program design.

- Re-evaluate periodically. Refer to your goals from time to time to see how you're doing.

- When you accomplish goals that you set, consider new ones.

Setting goals is a simple act, but it can play a big part in keeping your program interesting and challenging and keeping you motivated and involved.

RT Program Goals

Take a few minutes to think about what you would like to achieve from your RT program. Write down your goals in the space provided. Use the tips noted above as a guide.

Date _____

Start-Up Goals	Comments/Results
_____	_____
_____	_____
_____	_____
_____	_____

After an initial 10- to 12-week period, you may want to revise and update your goals. You can do this in the space below.

Date _____

Revise/New Goals	Comments/Results
_____	_____
_____	_____
_____	_____
_____	_____

2

FACTS AND FALLACIES

Those who spread misconceptions about resistance training should be sentenced to three 45-minute workouts per week until they discover the facts for themselves and admit the error of their ways.

Nine common misconceptions about RT are discussed in this chapter. Each fallacy is stated, followed by the facts of the matter to set the record straight.

Fallacy: *"You gain weight and get muscle-bound."*

Fact: You can gain weight through RT if you want to, but you don't have to. It depends on how you set up your program. People who gain considerable weight (by adding muscle mass) do so by using heavy weights and by training a couple of hours a day several days a week. And those who gain the most weight are those who have the largest muscle mass to begin with.

You may experience a minor weight gain in the early stages of your program. But if you follow the programs outlined here, you needn't be concerned about undue weight gain or about getting muscle-bound.

Fallacy: *"Strength training results in undesirable muscle development in women."*

Fact: Many highly competitive female athletes do become more muscular with training. It should be remembered, however, that they are usually the more athletic and muscular to begin with (which is why they excel in sport in the first place) and they train intensively for long periods each week.

The training programs outlined here are not of sufficient duration or intensity to result in unwarranted muscle development. Furthermore, women have less muscle mass and smaller quantities of testosterone (a male sex hormone which affects muscle growth) than men, so they can expect less muscle development than men for any given amount of RT.

While improving muscle tone by RT, some women find they actually lose weight and look better. This is especially true if the training is complemented by an endurance activity like running, cycling, or swimming. Thus, a regular exercise routine can lead to a favorable change in body composition: while muscle is being gained, fat is being lost. And since muscle is denser than fat (that is, a kilogram of muscle is *smaller* than a kilogram of fat) you can gain muscle and at the same time lose weight and inches.

Fallacy: *"Training makes you strong, but you also get slow and inflexible."*

Fact: Stronger, yes, but slower, no. In fact, studies show that there is a direct, positive relationship between strength and speed. Follow an appropriate RT routine and you get faster, not slower. That's why top-class sprinters and other athletes include it as a part of their overall conditioning program.

Now about the inflexible part. Go to a bodybuilding or weightlifting competition and watch the competitors warm-up. They're considerably more flexible than average. That's because they do a lot of flexibility exercises along with their weights. Anyone who loses flexibility while training with weights loses it not because of the weights, but because they devote insufficient time to stretching exercises.

A balanced RT program that uses the opposing muscle groups (agonists and antagonists) actually promotes flexibility. As one group of muscles (the agonists) work, the muscles that move the joint in the opposite direction (the antagonists) learn to relax.

Fallacy: *"Free weights are best!" "Universal equipment is best!" "Nautilus equipment is best!" And so on . . .*

Fact: We'll discuss the various types of equipment in the next chapter. For now, we'll simply say that there is a wide variety of excellent RT equipment available and that each type has its advantages and disadvantages depending on the goals and objectives of your program and the amount of time you have to devote to it. What's important is not the kind of equipment you use but how you use it. Using any reputable type of equipment, if you follow a proper program, you'll get results.

Fallacy: *"If it doesn't hurt, it's not doing any good!" (i.e., "No pain, no gain!")*

Fact: Those of the PTA (pain, torture, and agony) school of exercise raise their weary heads occasionally and expound such misconceptions as the ones above. Luckily, fewer and fewer people are listening.

When you begin an RT program you'll likely experience some minor stiffness and soreness. This is to be expected since your body is adapting to a new activity and your muscles will be working in ways they may not be used to. This start-up stiffness is OK if it's in the belly (middle) of the muscle, but not if the tendons at the ends of the muscles or the joints are sore.

RT, as we'll explain later, is based on the principle of *progressive overload.* For a safe and effective program, you should increase the intensity of your training slowly and comfortably over a period of time. You'll know you're progressing too quickly if you are tired or constantly stiff and sore after your training sessions. If you overdo it, you'll slow your progress, you may develop negative feelings about your program, and you increase your risk of injury.

Fallacy: *"If you want to build muscle mass and gain strength you have to consume large quantities of protein and take vitamin supplements."*

Fact: This one's a long-standing tradition in weight-lifting gyms of the world. Bodybuilders and other serious lifters have long contended that to get the most out of your training you have to consume extra quantities of foods containing protein (meat, eggs, cheese, etc.) and supplement the diet with vitamin pills and even protein drinks.

Research confirms there is an easier and less expensive way for active individuals to meet their energy and nutritional requirements. A well-balanced diet (as recommended in *Canada's Food Guide to Healthy Eating* and *USDA's Food Guide Pyramid* shown below) provides all the nutrients,

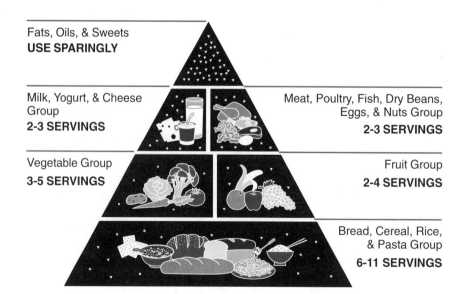

Fats, Oils, & Sweets
USE SPARINGLY

Milk, Yogurt, & Cheese Group
2-3 SERVINGS

Meat, Poultry, Fish, Dry Beans, Eggs, & Nuts Group
2-3 SERVINGS

Vegetable Group
3-5 SERVINGS

Fruit Group
2-4 SERVINGS

Bread, Cereal, Rice, & Pasta Group
6-11 SERVINGS

vitamins, and minerals the body requires. As your energy needs rise with increased activity, you simply increase your portion sizes slightly while maintaining a correct proportion of protein, carbohydrate, and fats.

This general increase in caloric consumption will take care of the active body's protein needs as well as its vitamin and mineral requirements. Remember that most excess vitamins and minerals are not stored in the body, but passed in the urine. Thus, supplementing can be both expensive and *wasteful.*

Fallacy: *"If you do certain exercises, you can lose weight in specific parts of the body."*

Fact: Not so. "Spot reduction" isn't possible. Certain exercises can increase muscle tone in specific areas, but they will not necessarily reduce fat in those areas. (Remember, muscle and fat are different tissues.)

Aerobic exercise and circuit training help "burn" fat, but the result will be a reduction in overall body fat, not reduced body fat in a particular area.

Fallacy: *"When you stop RT the muscle turns to fat."*

Fact: This is our favorite. It's also the easiest to disprove. Consider the following example. Someone breaks a leg skiing and the leg goes into a cast for several weeks or months to allow the broken bone(s) to heal. When the cast comes off, the muscles in that leg are now *smaller* than those in the other leg that has remained (somewhat) active in spite of the injury. (This difference in muscle size is easiest to see in the large thigh muscles.)

If muscle turned to fat, the leg just out of the cast would be less firm than the other leg but still the same size. It's not, though: The leg is smaller because the muscles have gotten smaller. The body fat level in the injured leg is the same as in the noninjured leg.

Simply stated, muscle and fat are different issues—different tissues. If muscle gets less activity (if you stop RT, for example), it atrophies or decreases in size. "Use it or lose it" is the phrase that best describes this process. While muscle doesn't change to fat through inactivity, if you become less active, you must modify your diet accordingly—consuming fewer calories—so that a gain in fat does not occur.

Fallacy: *"Resistance training is boring and it takes too much time."*

Fact: We've always contended that boredom is self-inflicted. If your RT becomes boring—if your routine becomes a rut— you have to change it so you enjoy it again. Use this book as it's designed, and your routine can be interesting, challenging, and fun for a long time to come.

RT needn't take too much time, either. Some serious athletes spend a great deal of time at it, but they have to and they usually want to. If you're training for health, fitness, or for some recreational activity, you only need two or three brief sessions each week. And if you don't dally you can get a good workout in 30 to 45 minutes.

3

STRONG
TERMS

Before we launch into the art
and science of resistance training, we should set out some of
the key terms and definitions.

Background terms and "working words" are covered first.
These terms all appear in the index as well, so if you come
across something later and you can't quite remember what's
what, you can return here to refresh your memory.

The final section of the chapter includes a "muscle map"
depicting the major muscle groups in the body. This will help
you understand which muscles are used in the different
exercises.

BACKGROUND TERMS

We know there is nothing more off-putting than people who overwhelm you with a barrage of techno-babble about their favorite subject. Still, learning a new fitness skill is a little like visiting an exotic country: You may not need to learn the native language, but it sure helps to learn enough phrases to get directions. Here, then, is a concise phrase book for the background terms associated with RT: strength, power and muscle endurance; types of exercises; and types of equipment.

RESISTANCE TRAINING (RT) DEFINED

Resistance training is any exercise where you are working against some source of resistance. The resistance could be as simple as your own body weight or as sophisticated as the latest training equipment.

STRENGTH, POWER, AND MUSCULAR ENDURANCE TERMINOLOGY

By definition, strength is the maximum force that muscles can exert under static (i.e., no movement) conditions. For discussion and training purposes, strength is usually considered in three sub-categories: strength, power, and muscular endurance.

Strength (compared to power and muscular endurance) is the maximum force that can be exerted in a single, all-out effort. The competitive weight lifter must rely on strength.

Power implies explosive action or the ability of a muscle to exert force with speed. The volleyball player or high jumper must respond quickly. Power is important for them.

Muscular endurance is the ability of a muscle to contract repeatedly or to sustain a contraction against moderate resistance. Muscular endurance is important in activities like running and cross-country skiing. It is also required in many of our daily activities.

Programs can be designed to emphasize the development of strength, power, or muscular endurance, with the emphasis determined by your own goals and objectives.

TERMS ASSOCIATED WITH TYPES OF EXERCISES

You've probably heard something about isometric or isotonic exercises. Strictly speaking, isometric and isotonic properly refer only to internal muscle effort. By convention, however, the terms isometric, isotonic, and isokinetic are used to describe various types of exercises, as follows.

Isometric exercises are those in which the muscles exert force against an immovable resistance (pushing out with the hands on a door frame, for example) and where there is no change in muscle length during contraction. Isometrics were all the rage in the late 1950s and early 1960s. But it was soon found that the range of possible exercises was limited and that routines could become boring. Isometrics are still used a great deal in the initial stages of therapeutic exercise and in rehabilitation, but they are less popular now in general RT programs.

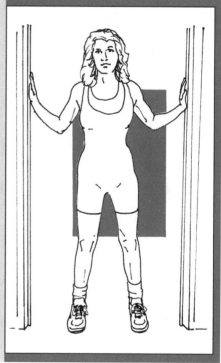

Isotonic exercises are those in which there is a change in muscle length as a resistance (a barbell, for example) is moved through a range of motion. The weight of the barbell is constant, obviously, but it is easier to lift during certain stages of the range of motion. This is due to physics and joint mechanics and to the number of muscle fibers that can be activated at different points in the range of motion. The exercise feels easier when the number of muscle fibers being used is greater and/or when the mechanics of the motion are more efficient (near the top of a biceps curl, for example).

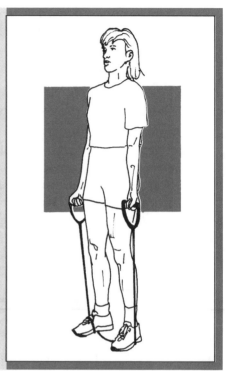

Isokinetic exercises are performed on specialized equipment. As with isotonic exercise, a resistance (weight) is moved through a range of motion. However, in an isokinetic exercise, the *speed* of movement is controlled by the equipment, and it offers "accommodating resistance." We talk more about this when dealing with guided-resistance equipment.

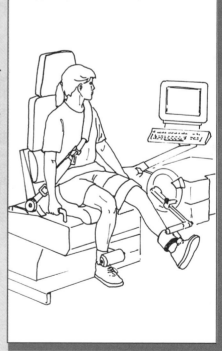

TERMS ASSOCIATED WITH TYPES OF EQUIPMENT

There is a variety of RT equipment available. This section provides some details on the main types.

Free weight equipment includes all types of barbells and dumbbells, as well as accessory items like benches and racks to assist with the various exercises. Free weights are inexpensive; for relatively little cost, you can organize your own RT area at home. They're also versatile, allowing for a wide variety of exercises.

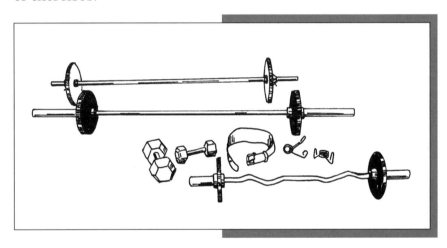

Guided-resistance equipment relies on a **lever arm** to guide your body (or part of it) through a particular movement pattern. Resistance is provided by a "**weight stack**" or other mechanical-resistance apparatus attached to the lever arm.

Guided-resistance equipment may consist of single stations or multiple stations grouped together around a central core. This type of equipment is quick and easy to use. To change the resistance on a weight-stack machine, you simply reposition a pin. Guided-resistance equipment is generally considered to be safer and more comfortable to use than free weights since there are no weights to drop, your movements are guided (or controlled) by the lever arm, and solid support is provided for your body in a variety of body positions. A seated chest press machine is shown here.

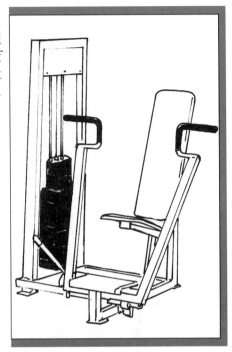

Variable resistance equipment is a type of guided-resistance equipment that provides resistance, which varies as you follow the range of motion. Variable resistance is accomplished on weight-stack and air-cylinder machines through the use of levers, **elliptical cams**, or other devices. These machines are an attempt to provide a more effective workout by offering *more* resistance in the range where we are stronger and less resistance where we are not as strong.

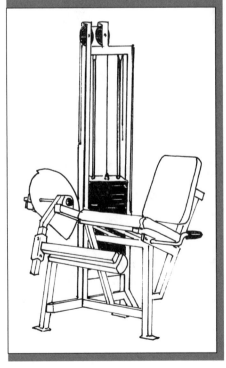

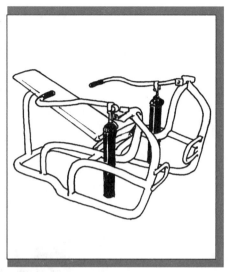

Accommodating resistance machines (**hydraulic** or electromagnetic) are more sophisticated guided-resistance systems that react to the user and provide resistance that matches the user's ability to generate force at all points in the range of motion. That is, the harder you push or pull, the greater the resistance provided by the machine. Where you are less strong, you get less resistance. Some of these machines control the movement speed (isokinetic); others allow you to work within a given speed range (omni-kinetic). This type of system can be very effective. It is also very safe since you are never faced with a load that you can't handle.

In this book we include exercises performed with free weights and with weight-stack equipment. These two types of equipment are now widely available in schools, community recreation center, YMCAs and YWCAs, and fitness clubs. It is important to note that the exercises and programs discussed here can be applied to *any* type of equipment.

WORKING WORDS

The following terms are commonly used in describing RT programs. Because they are concise terms they allow exercise descriptions to be brief and straightforward. To complement some of the definitions we have provided examples from the exercises included in the book. Refer to the exercises mentioned as you work your way through the definitions if it will help clarify things for you. These "working words" are used frequently throughout the remainder of the book, so refer to this section later if you need to refresh your memory.

BODY POSITIONS

There are two body positions involved.

Prone means lying face down (on your front), as for the push-up.

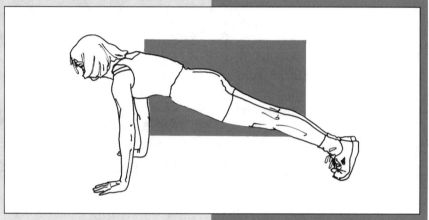

Supine means lying face up (on your back), as in the chest press.

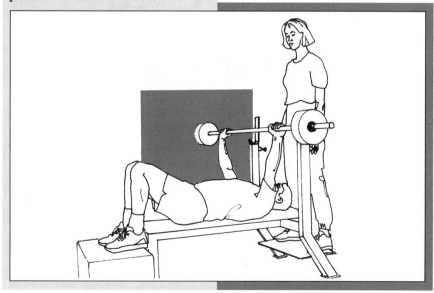

Adduction is the action of drawing toward—when a limb moves toward the mid-line of the body, as in the hip adduction.

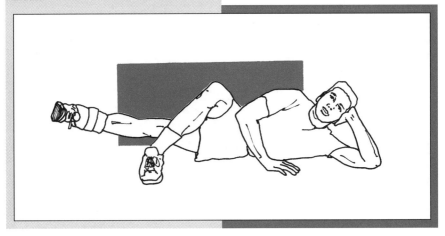

Abduction is the action of taking away or moving a limb away from the mid-line of the body, as in the side leg raise.

Finally, a couple of ankle motions that sound a little complicated, but are not really.

Dorsiflexion occurs when the ankle is flexed, pointing the toes *up* and *toward* the knee, as in the shin pull.

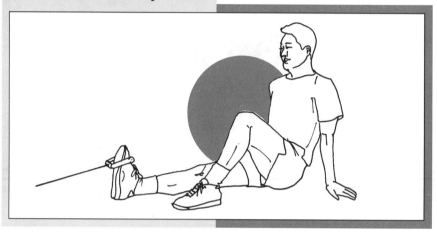

Plantarflexion occurs when the ankle is flexed, pointing the toes *away* from the knee, as in the calf raise.

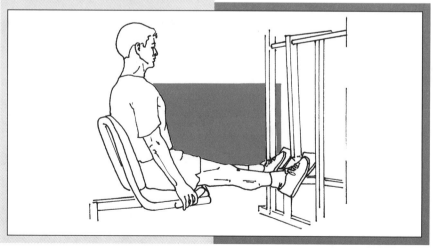

Two types of muscle action occur to bring about the motions just described. In **concentric contraction** the muscle *shortens* while it exerts force. In **eccentric contraction** it *lengthens* while it exerts force. Most RT exercises include both concentric and eccentric contraction of the involved muscles.

THE ACTORS

During any strength exercise, various muscles play different roles. Some of these roles are major, other are minor.

Prime movers are muscles directly responsible for producing a given action.

Assistant movers are muscles which play a secondary role, aiding the prime movers in producing a desired movement.

Stabilizers are muscles which help maintain the proper body position and prohibit undesirable movement during execution of an exercise.

Take the half squat exercise, for example:

- the spinal erectors and abdominals serve as stabilizers;

- the quadriceps and gluteals are the prime movers; and

- the hamstrings are assistant movers.

THE VARIABLES

There are several variables you can work with: resistance, repetitions, sets, and the rest interval. Change any of these variables and you alter the intensity of your program. We'll discuss how to work with these variables in the next chapter. For now, here are the definitions:

The *resistance* is the weight or load that a muscle works against.

A *repetition* (rep) is the single, complete action of an exercise from starting position to completion and back to the starting position.

A *set* consists of a given number of complete and continuous repetitions of an exercise.

The *rest interval* is the amount of rest/recovery taken between sets of an exercise or between different exercises in a program.

Thus, 10 uninterrupted repetitions of an exercise give you one set of 10. Rest a minute or two and do 10 more reps. You've now done two sets of 10, and so on. The common short form for recording workouts is as follows:

Chest press	3 × 12	(40)	2
(exercise)	(sets) × (reps)	(resistance or weight in kilograms)	(rest interval in minutes)

The type of routine you do and the order in which you do the exercises will also affect the intensity of your program. These variables are explained in the next chapter.

MUSCLE MAP

This "muscle map" depicts the body's major muscles and muscle groups—those playing the biggest part in the RT exercises beginning in Chapter 6. The map is in no way complete. We have purposely omitted some of the smaller muscles, feeling that they added unnecessary detail and would simply impair clarity.

The names of some muscles have common short forms, and we use the short forms throughout this book. In such cases, we have included the muscle's formal name in parentheses.

Included with each exercise in Chapter 6 through 9 is a list of the muscles used. For simplicity we have grouped the stabilizing, flexion, and extension muscles on either side of the spine under the term "paraspinals." You may wish to refer to this map to clarify the muscles in question as you work your way through the various exercises.

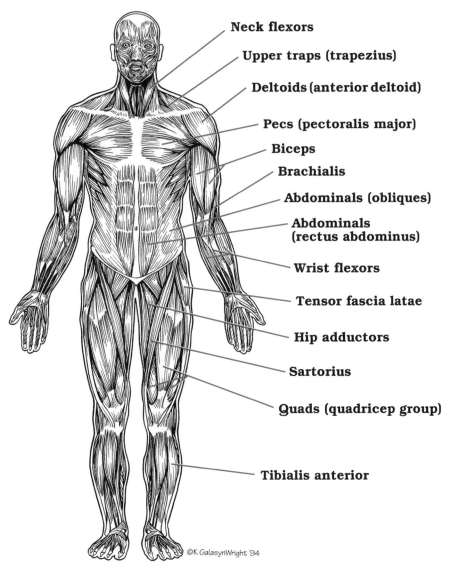

Neck flexors

Upper traps (trapezius)

Deltoids (anterior deltoid)

Pecs (pectoralis major)

Biceps

Brachialis

Abdominals (obliques)

Abdominals
(rectus abdominus)

Wrist flexors

Tensor fascia latae

Hip adductors

Sartorius

Quads (quadricep group)

Tibialis anterior

©K GalasynWright '94

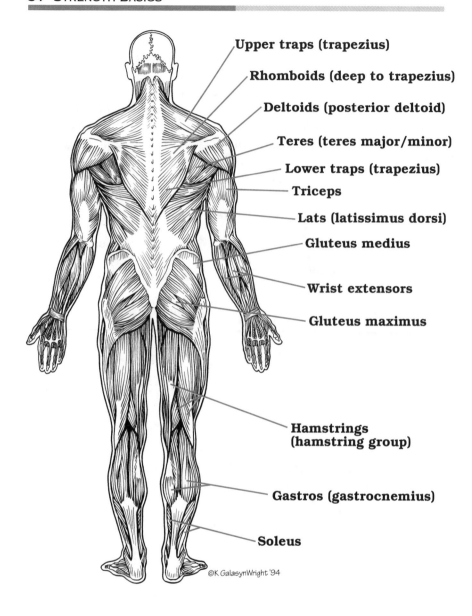

Upper traps (trapezius)

Rhomboids (deep to trapezius)

Deltoids (posterior deltoid)

Teres (teres major/minor)

Lower traps (trapezius)

Triceps

Lats (latissimus dorsi)

Gluteus medius

Wrist extensors

Gluteus maximus

Hamstrings
(hamstring group)

Gastros (gastrocnemius)

Soleus

©K GalasynWright '94

4

DESIGNING YOUR PROGRAM

This chapter explains how various components of a program fit together and why they fit together the way they do. It explains how often and how long you should train, how to choose and arrange your exercises, how to find your starting weights, and how to progress. It also considers the program focus and provides tips to help you stick with your program when you've been at it for a while. An understanding of these guidelines will provide a firm foundation for your RT routine.

The final section of the chapter offers some tips for purchasing RT equipment. This will be helpful if you would like to train in the comfort and convenience of your own home.

FORMATTING YOUR ROUTINE

Bodybuilders, weight lifters, and some athletes (shot putters, for example) may train as often as six days a week for two or three hours each session. Other serious athletes may do three or four sessions a week, each session lasting as long as one and a half or two hours. The nature of the sport and the stage of the athlete's training cycle determine the emphasis placed on RT training.

Individuals training for health and fitness or using RT to condition for a favorite sport needn't work out as often or as long as the serious lifter or athlete. Two or three sessions a week is quite adequate. Greater progress is realized with a thrice-weekly program, but twice a week is just fine if it complements your other activities. And, as mentioned in Chapter 2, you can get in a good workout in 30 to 45 minutes.

Chart 4.1 on page 38 shows typical routine formats—the *frequency* and *duration* of sessions—for heavy strength training, athletic training, and beginning training for health and fitness or conditioning for recreational sports.

Routine Format

Decide on

- frequency (the number of sessions per week), and

- duration (the length of each session).

Recommended for beginners and for training for health and fitness: 30 to 45 minutes, two to three times a week.

ROUTINE TYPE

There are two considerations: whether a routine is a circuit or regular and whether a standard or a variable system is used with respect to the program variables mentioned in Chapter 2.

CIRCUIT OR REGULAR?

In *circuit training* you do the first set of the first exercise, the first set of the second exercise, the first set of the third exercise, and so on through to the last exercise. You then return to the first exercise and go through the sequence again. Two or three circuits of 10 exercises (i.e., 2 × 12 or 3 × 12) is a typical routine.

Sometimes circuit training is done with a series of minicircuits. A circuit consisting of nine exercises could, for example, be broken down into three minicircuits of three exercises. If you're doing two sets of 10 reps, you would finish your 2 × 10 of the first group of three exercises before moving on to the second group. This approach adds variety to a program and it also helps you adhere more strictly to the "Ordering Exercises" guideline explained below.

In a *regular routine* you concentrate on one exercise at a time. That is, if you're doing a 3 × 10 program, you complete all three sets of the first exercise before moving on to the second exercise. Since the same muscle groups are exercised three times in succession, more rest is required between sets in a regular routine than in a circuit. Therefore, more time is required to complete any given exercise session.

STANDARD OR VARIABLE?

In a *standard routine*, the resistance, reps and sets, and length of rest interval do not vary during any given workout. An example of a standard chest-press series would be three sets of 10 repetitions, all at 50 kg (3 × 10 [50]).

In a *variable routine*, for any exercise, the resistance, the number of reps or sets, or the rest interval may vary during the workout. One type of variable routine, using four sets of the chest press, for example, could consist of 10 reps at 60 kilograms, 8 × 70 kg, 6 × 75 kg, and 4 × 80 kg. Variable routines can get rather complicated and are beyond the scope of this book.

Typically, RT programs for health and fitness or for conditioning for recreational sports are circuit routines following the standard approach. They are efficient, effective, and less time-consuming or complicated than regular and/or variable routines.

Routine Type

Choose a

■ circuit or regular sequence of exercises, and

■ standard or variable combination of reps, sets, resistance, and rest intervals.

Recommended for beginners and for training for health and fitness: Standard, circuit. It's simple, quick, and efficient!

Chart 4.1 shows the types of programs generally used by those with different weight training goals and objectives.

Chart 4.1 Formats and Types of Resistance Training Programs				
Goal/Objective	Format		Type	
	Frequency (days/week)	Duration (time/session)	Circuit or regular	Standard or variable
Heavy strength training	5–6	2 hours or more	regular	both
Training for competitive athletes	3–4	3/4 hour– 1 1/2 hours	both	both
Training for health and fitness or conditioning for recreational sports	2–3	1/2 hour– 3/4 hour	circuit	standard

SELECTING EXERCISES

Your program should include a wide variety of exercises to ensure adequate *overall development.* The routines in this book adhere to this principle: each one includes exercises for the shoulders, arms, chest, torso, and legs.

It is also important that a routine achieve *balanced development.* Balanced development means that opposing muscles are given appropriate attention. That is, when you work the biceps, you must also work the triceps. Exercise the gastroc and soleus, and you should exercise the tibialis anterior. (See the "muscle map" in Chapter 3 if you wish to clarify where these muscles are located).

The development of opposing muscle groups should be looked at another way, as well. The endurance of particular muscles is enhanced through specific activities. Quad development occurs in cycling, for example, while running strengthens the muscles down the back of the body (i.e., the spinal erectors, hamstrings, gastroc, and soleus). RT can be used to strengthen the muscles opposing those that are most involved in other activities and, thus, help maintain a proper balance of strength. The cyclist can do hamstring exercises and the runner can perform exercises to strengthen the muscles down the front—the abdominals, quads, and tibialis anterior.

The balanced development principle applies to body parts as well as opposing muscle groups. You should not concentrate on upper body development, for example, by including an array of exercises for the arms and chest while including none for the legs.

To ensure balanced development, then, you must consider the goals and objectives of your program and the muscle strengthening that occurs in your other activities, then select your exercises accordingly.

If your RT program is mainly to condition for a sport, you'll eventually want to include some exercises specific to the actions and activities of the sport. Chapter 10 covers sport-specific training in detail.

Exercise Selection

Do a combination of exercises that offers

- good overall development,

- balanced development of body parts and opposing muscle groups, and

- preparation for (and a complement to) your other activities.

Recommended for beginners and for training for health and fitness: A general program covering all major muscle groups.

ORDERING EXERCISES

When training for health and fitness or for recreational activities, the exercises should be ordered to provide a *work-rest effect* for muscles or body parts. An upper-body exercise followed by a leg exercise followed by an abdominal exercise adheres to this principle. The upper body "rests" while the legs are exercised, and so on. This same work-rest principle would have a triceps exercise follow a biceps exercise, for example; never would two exercises for the same muscle group follow one after another.

Arrange your exercises properly, and your circuit-training routine can be quite efficient. Examine the core routines in Chapter 8—they are set up to follow the work-rest principle (by body part), which means you can move fairly quickly from one exercise to the next, resting one body part while another part works. You save time (compared to a regular routine) because you never have to pause for a total rest.

Another aspect of this principle says that total body exercises or exercises requiring balance and coordination (the clean or bench step-up, for example) should be done early in a session, before fatigue builds. For the same reason, exercises for the larger, stronger muscle groups (requiring more resistance) should also be completed early in your program or near the beginning of a series of exercises for a given body area. This is obviously difficult to do in a circuit-training program. However, these latter considerations are more related to programs for athletic training, which usually follow a regular, not a circuit, routine.

Exercise Order

■ Follow the work-rest principle.

Recommended for beginners and for training for health and fitness: Order the exercises by body part in a work-then-rest sequence.

FINDING YOUR STARTING WEIGHTS

Some people like to start an RT program using free weights or weight-stack equipment by testing themselves the first day. They might lift heavy weights to determine their maximum in each exercise or do fast repetitions with light weights for a specified period of time (30 seconds or a minute, for example). Their test results are then used to establish the starting resistance and reps for their routine.

For reasons that may seem obvious, we do not recommend any of these methods. It takes time to learn proper technique. First-day, all-out efforts risk injury and are sure to cause undue stiffness and soreness. It's just not worth it!

Instead, we favor a more casual approach. Start with a resistance that seems too light. Experiment to find the load that allows you to do your sets and reps comfortably and with proper technique.

It's easy to experiment if you're using weight-stack equipment, which has supporting pins for the weight stacks. Have a partner move the pin for you while you stay in position for the exercise and do different levels of resistance (a rep or two or each) until you find the load that's right for you. This same experimental approach takes a little longer using barbells or dumbbells, but you should follow it nonetheless.

A gradual, sensible beginning to RT is just as important as it is in any other aspect of a fitness regimen. Injuries and setbacks await those who try for too much, too soon.

Getting Started

- Learn proper technique.

- Use light weights and experiment.

- Increase resistance gradually.

- Go for comfort.

Recommended for beginners: Be sensible. Follow the advice above. Avoid testing or maximum, all-out efforts.

MAKING PROGRESS

If you wish to improve (i.e., get stronger), you must follow the principle of *progressive overload*. That is, as your body adapts to the demands placed upon it, you must increase those demands if you wish to continue improving.

This is where the variables introduced in Chapter 3 come into play. By increasing the resistance or the number of sets or reps, or decreasing the rest interval, you can make your routine more demanding.

As with starting, there is nothing terribly scientific about how you should progress. Slowly and gradually is the only way to go. A simple example is the best way to demonstrate proper progression.

Let's say your RT is a part of an overall fitness program of two or three sessions a week to complement commuting by bicycle to and from work. Chart 4.2 on page 44 recommends two to four sets of 8 to 12 or more repetitions of each exercise. Since you've recently found your starting weights and you're still learning proper technique, you should be working at the low end of the range—two sets of 10 repetitions.

You do 2 × 10 for a while and it gets too easy. So, you add a couple more reps of each exercise. Now you're at 2 × 12. After a while, it gets easy again, so you go to 2 × 13, then 2 × 14, and eventually 2 × 15.

Now you drop it back to 12 reps and, at the same time, add a third set. You do the same for a few more sessions. Next, you increase the resistance and drop the reps back to 10. Then you slowly move the reps back up to 15 again—and so on.

Please note that this is only one way to progress. There are many different ways to change the resistance/reps/sets/rest interval combinations to increase the demands of your program. Follow the approach that feels right for you, but be sure to:

- Increase your reps or sets for a while before increasing the resistance. Remember, you should be using light resistance in the early stages while you're learning proper technique.

- Increase only one variable at a time, otherwise the immediate increase in the total volume of your workout could be substantial.

- Decrease the reps slightly when you add another set of each exercise. Note that if you go from 2×10 to 3×10, you have had an immediate 50 percent increase in the amount of work. Instead, if you worked up to 2×15 and then went to 3×12 (sets up, reps down), you've only had a 20 percent increase.

- Take into account the size of the muscles you are using when you are ready to increase the resistance. In general, you should use a smaller increase for upper-body exercises (i.e., 5 lb./2.5 kg. or more) compared to the larger, stronger leg muscles (10 lb./5 kg. or more).

You might also standardize your rest interval. Take just enough time to go comfortably from one exercise to the next, but without delay or wasting any time. You can, however, work on decreasing your rest interval and keeping it to a bare minimum if you want your routine to be a more demanding cardiovascular/muscular endurance workout.

Progressing

- Follow the principle of progressive overload.

- Change reps, sets, resistance, and rest interval gradually to increase the demands of your program.

Recommended for beginners and for training for health and fitness: Easy does it!

FOCUSING YOUR PROGRAM

The concepts of heavy strength training, athletic training, and training for health and fitness or conditioning for recreational sports were introduced early in this chapter in the section "Routine Format." The frequency and duration of training sessions depend on the type of training being pursued. Frequency and duration are dealt with in Chart 4.1 on page 38, making it is easy to see how these types of training differ.

The program focus relates to these three types of training and any specific sport or occupational activity that may be the reason for RT. Together, they will determine whether the program should focus on developing strength or power or muscular endurance. The focus, in turn, will establish the appropriate program variables: reps, sets, resistance, and rest interval.

These are set out in Chart 4.2. Generally, a low-repetition, heavy resistance program is used to develop muscle size and strength; a high-repetition, light-resistance routine improves muscle definition and muscular endurance. Program focus comes heavily into play in Chapter 10, where sport-specific RT routines are discussed.

Chart 4.2	Variables for Designing Resistance Training Programs			
Focus	**Repetitions**	**Sets**	**Resistance[1]**	**Rest Interval**
Strength	1 - 4	4 - 8	85% -100%	2 - 4 minutes
Power	5 - 8	3 - 6	70% - 80%	1 1/2 - 2 minutes
Muscular endurance	8 - 12 or more[2]	2 - 4	50% - 70%	45 - 90 seconds

[1] The percentages noted in this column are percents of the maximum load you can lift for only one repetition. We've listed these figures merely to give you an idea of the *relative* loads you should use in order to emphasize the development of strength or power or muscular endurance. Some weeks or months into your programs, if you're doing 2 to 4 sets of 8 to 12 reps for example, you will be doing them with the loads in the range of 50% to 70% of the maximum weight you could do for one rep. In a backward sort of way, then, you can estimate your maximums for various exercises based on the load you're using for your sets and reps.

[2] Start by doing 8 reps of each exercise. When you've been at your program for a while, use fewer reps for upper-body exercises (8-12, for example) and more for leg exercises (15-20, say). This is where the "or more" comes into play. It also applies for exercises such as curl-ups. Some people end up doing sets of 25, 30, or more curl-ups later on into their programs.

Most readers of this book will want to pursue a routine that focuses on developing muscular endurance. Chart 4.2 tells you what you should do to accomplish this.

Focus

■ Determine the objectives of your program.

■ Decide whether the focus should be on developing strength, power, or muscular endurance.

■ Establish the appropriate reps, sets, resistance, and rest interval.

Recommended for beginners and for training for health and fitness: Focus on muscular endurance, doing two to four sets of 8 to 12 reps or more, with light to moderate resistance and short rest intervals (45 to 90 seconds between reps and sets).

MAINTAINING YOUR PROGRAM

In the early stages of your program—when you're getting started—motivation shouldn't be a problem. Things will be new, you'll be experiencing fairly rapid gains, and you'll be enthusiastic about your progress.

After a while, though, you may want to continue gaining strength, but you'll hit plateaus or sticking points where, for a number of workouts or weeks, you don't improve. This is when the advice on motivation in Chapter 5 will help out.

Later on, you will have found your favorite exercises and learned how long and how often you want to train. This is the time for program maintenance, a time when you have no need or desire to become stronger, but simply want to maintain what you've gained.

At this point, you'll want to make sure your program remains interesting and enjoyable. Be sure to retain your favorite exercises, but vary the others, substituting appropriate exercises in the Chapter 9 catalogue for those in your current routine. Or, you could change your routine entirely. If you're doing one of the routines in Chapter 8, for example, you could switch to the routine in Chapters 6 or 7 for a while.

Sticking With Your Program

■ Retain favorite exercises from your regular routine.

■ Substitute or add new exercises from the Chapter 9 catalogue.

■ Vary your program to keep it interesting and challenging.

Program Design Summary

In a nutshell, here are all of the guidelines for proper program design covered in this chapter.

If you're a beginner, and/or training for health and fitness:

■ Do two to three sessions per week, of 30 to 45 minutes each.

■ Follow a standard, circuit routine.

■ Select exercises to give balanced, overall development.

■ Order the exercises to adhere to the work-rest principle.

■ Start with light weights and learn proper technique.

■ Increase the demands of your program gradually.

■ Emphasize the development of muscular endurance. Do two to four sets of 8 to 12 or more reps, with light to moderate resistance and 45- to 90-second rests between reps and sets.

■ When you feel the need, vary your program to keep it interesting. Draw on the Chapter 9 exercises to do this.

EQUIPMENT FOR HOME USE

If RT in the comfort of your own home sounds appealing, you don't have to break the bank to get started. Here are some things to consider when purchasing equipment for home use.

MINOR EQUIPMENT, ACCESSORIES, AND TUBING

Body-weight exercises (like those in Chapter 6) can be made more demanding by adding an external resistance. You can improvise here if you like. You could, for example, drape your telephone directory across your knee in the side leg raise (p.72). Just go easy if you live in Chicago, Toronto, New York, or L.A.! Or, you could hold (full) juice tins in your hands for the calf raise (page 78) and half squat (page 79).

To accomplish the same thing (perhaps more comfortably), you can purchase light weights, which you hold in your hands or strap to your wrist or around your leg. In the case of strap-on or soft weights, look for items with a soft exterior and an easy, secure method to fasten them (Velcro, for example).

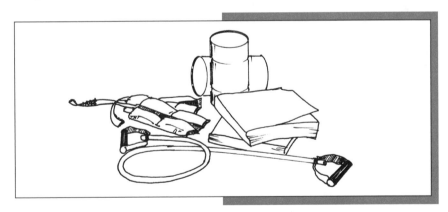

If the tubing routine in Chapter 7 suits your style, you should be on your way for about $10 to $20. Tubing can be purchased in a kit, with handles attached, or in bulk. If you buy it in bulk, we recommend a 12-foot length. You can tie a loop at each end to make a handle, and a piece this length allows for a wide variety of exercises. Tubing exercise kits and bulk tubing can be found in many sporting goods stores. Bulk tubing can also be found at medical, rehabilitation, or pharmaceutical supply stores. Look for tubing with a wall thickness of 1.5 to 3 mm. and an overall diameter of 1.0 to 1.5 cm.

FREE WEIGHTS

Keep your free-weight equipment simple and versatile. Start with a barbell, dumbbells, and a bench, and add other equipment later if you wish.

Look for a barbell and dumbbells with inner movable sleeves which you grip and outside collars which secure the weight plates on the bar. Removable weight plates allow you to change the load as you move from one exercise to the next and to add weight as you progress and get stronger.

Steel bars and cast-iron plates are your best bet. Plates with a cement-type filling and vinyl outer cover are quieter when you set them down, but are more susceptible to breakage if you happen to drop them. Hey, it happens!

Get a bench that's long enough for you to lie down on for the chest press (see page 99) and the proper height for you to do the leg exercises that require a bench. (You can also use it for the exercises done sitting down.) Be sure the bench is sturdy. If you're skilled and so inclined, you can make your own bench. If you're going to do this, visit a local fitness facility and measure their benches—then get building!

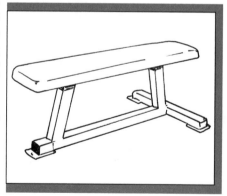

HOME GYMS/STACK WEIGHTS

Mini versions of the stack-weight equipment common at fitness facilities can be purchased for home use. (If you can't sleep some night, you can get up and surf the infomercial channels on TV for the latest in home gyms.)

The better machines have one weight stack providing resistance for many exercise stations. They also allow you to change exercises by simply changing your body position or using a different station. You shouldn't have to change cables or lever arms, or reconfigure the machine.

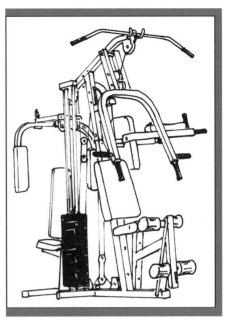

RT equipment can be purchased at sporting goods stores, the sports section of department stores, and at specialty fitness equipment stores. You could also check the classified ads in your local newspaper for used equipment.

Purchasing Home Equipment

Here are a few tips for equipment selection—especially free weights and the more expensive products. First, establish your price range and decide what features are important to you. Then:

- Try it before you buy it.

- If you'll have to sit or stand on it, make sure it's comfortable.

- Look for an accompanying manual with assembly instruction (if needed) and guidelines for use.

- If buying new equipment, expect a reasonable warranty, easy maintenance, and available service if required.

- Pick higher quality, more durable equipment.

If you choose equipment carefully and buy what suits you, it should serve you well for a long time.

5

PLAYING
IT SAFE,
HAVING FUN

This chapter covers safety and motivation. It includes a simple questionnaire to complete before you begin, advice for injury prevention and safety, and tips for sticking with your program.

PRE-EXERCISE CLEARANCE

If you're quite inactive now, complete Chart 5.1, the *PAR-Q and You* physical activity readiness questionnaire, before you start your resistance training program. Read it carefully, answer the questions, and follow the "yes" or "no" advice, whichever applies to you.

RT (especially exercises involving the upper body) places strong demands on the heart and may be inappropriate for some people, such as those with heart problems or high blood pressure. A health concern won't necessarily exclude you from participating, however; in fact, many cardio-respiratory rehabilitation programs and other therapeutic applications include RT as part of the recovery and health promotion prescription. Talk to your doctor if you have any doubts. Then see a fitness specialist if you need some help to fine-tune your program.

Chart 5.1 PAR-Q & YOU

(A Questionnaire for People Aged 15 to 69)

Regular physical activity is fun and healthy, and increasingly more people are starting to become more active every day. Being more active is very safe for most people. However, some people should check with their doctors before they start becoming much more physically active.

If you are planning to become much more physically active than you are now, start by answering the seven questions below. If you are between the ages of 15 and 69, the PAR-Q will tell you if you should check with your doctor before you start. If you are over 69 years of age, and you are not used to being very active, check with your doctor.

Common sense is your best guide when you answer these questions. Please read the questions carefully and answer each one honestly: Check YES or NO.

YES NO

☐ ☐ 1. Has your doctor ever said that you have a heart condition *and* that you should only do physical activity recommended by a doctor?

☐ ☐ 2. Do you feel pain in your chest when you do physical activity?

☐ ☐ 3. In the past month, have you had chest pain when you were not doing physical activity?

☐ ☐ 4. Do you lose your balance because of dizziness or do you ever lose consciousness?

❏ ❏ 5. Do you have a bone or joint problem that could be made worse by a change in your physical activity?

❏ ❏ 6. Is your doctor currently prescribing drugs (for example, water pills) for your blood pressure or heart condition?

❏ ❏ 7. Do you know of <u>any other reason</u> why you should not do physical activity?

IF YOU ANSWERED <u>YES</u> TO ONE OR MORE QUESTIONS

Talk with your doctor by phone or in person BEFORE you start becoming much more physically active or BEFORE you have a fitness appraisal. Tell your doctor about the PAR-Q and which questions you answered YES.

■ You may be able to do any activity you want—as long as you start slowly and build up gradually. Or, you may need to restrict your activities to those that are safe for you. Talk with your doctor about the kinds of activities you wish to participate in and follow his/her advice.

■ Find out which community programs are safe and helpful for you.

IF YOU ANSWERED <u>NO</u> TO ALL QUESTIONS

If you answered NO honestly to <u>all</u> PAR-Q questions, you can be reasonably sure that you can

■ start becoming much more physically active—begin slowly and build up gradually. This is the safest and easiest way to go.

■ take part in a fitness appraisal—this is an excellent way to determine your basic fitness so that you can plan the best way for you to live actively.

DELAY BECOMING MUCH MORE ACTIVE:

■ if you are not feeling well because of a temporary illness such as a cold or a fever—wait until you feel better; or

■ if you are or may be pregnant—talk to your doctor before you start becoming more active.

Please note: If your health changes so that you then answer YES to any of the above questions, tell your fitness or health professional. Ask whether you should change your physical activity plan.
*Reprinted by special permission from the Canadian Society for Exercise Physiology, Inc. Copyright 1994, CSEP.

INJURY PREVENTION AND SAFETY

Heed the following guidelines for trouble-free RT.

WARM-UP

A good warm-up increases heart rate and body temperature, stretches connective tissue at the ends of the muscles, and helps lubricate the joints. Warming up before your RT program will give you greater ease and freedom of movement and reduce your risk of injury.

Start with a few minutes of light aerobic activity (brisk walking, easy jogging, cycling, stepping, etc.). Follow this with some gentle stretching exercises. Use The Stretch Bit routine if you like.

THE STRETCH BIT

To get the most from your warm-up stretching routine:

- Stretch slowly and smoothly without bouncing or jerking.
- Strive for a stretched, relaxed feeling. Avoid pain—it means you're stretching too far.
- Breathe in a natural rhythm. Don't hold your breath.
- Use a gentle, *continuous* movement for the first and last exercises. Start with 10 repetitions (with each arm).
- Use a *stretch-and-hold* movement for all other exercises. Start with four repetitions of each one, holding the stretched position for 10 seconds minimum (and resting between reps). Later on, hold the position longer—15 to 20 seconds or more—and add repetitions if you want to stretch even more.
- Be sure to repeat the movement on both sides of the body to ensure a balanced routine.
- Avoid exercises that hurt or feel uncomfortable.

SINGLE ARM CIRCLE

Full, slow, sweeping circles with one arm. Forward, then backward. Repeat the sequence with your other arm.

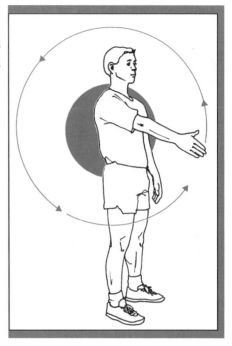

SIDE STRETCH

Reach one arm down the outside of the leg, leaving the other arm hanging comfortably at your side. Repeat the sequence on the other side.

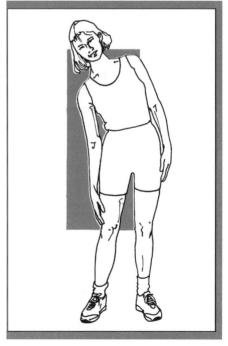

TRUNK TWIST

With knees slightly bent, trunk twist slowly in one direction, reaching the arm behind and looking back, while placing the other arm across the stomach. Twist alternately in the opposite direction.

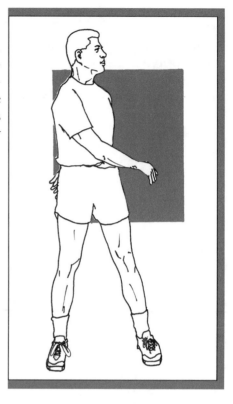

SIT-REACH

Sit with one leg straight, toes pointed up, and one leg bent with the sole of the foot near the knee of straight leg. Reach out along your straight leg. Next, change positions so the other leg is straight and repeat.

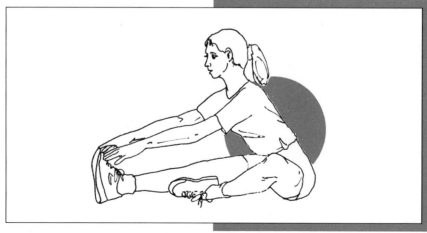

SIDE-TO-SIDE

Seat yourself with your legs in front, knees bent, feet flat on the floor. Roll legs to one side toward the floor. Look over the other shoulder. Repeat the stretch, rolling your legs to the other side and looking over the opposite shoulder.

LOW BACK STRETCH

On your back, grasp your hands behind one knee, and bring it toward your chest. Return that leg to the floor and repeat the stretch using the other leg.

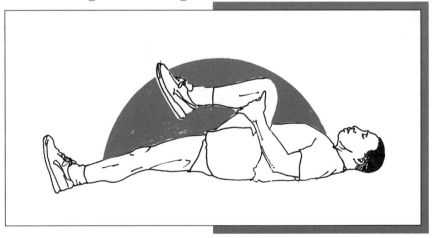

SPLIT STRETCH

Stand with your legs apart, feet pointing straight ahead. Shift weight over one leg, keeping the other leg straight and both feet flat on the floor. Next, shift your weight over the other leg.

THIGH STRETCH

Bend one knee, grasp your ankle, and pull your foot gently toward the buttock. Keep the supporting leg slightly bent and the back erect. Use a chair for support if you like. Repeat alternately with the other leg.

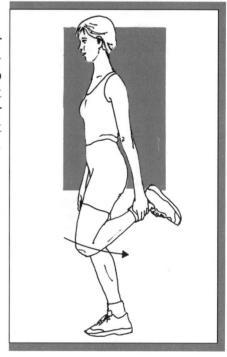

SOLEUS STRETCH

Standing with one foot in front of the other and your feet pointing straight ahead, bend both legs (squatting) to stretch the muscle in the lower part of the rear leg. Repeat with legs repositioned to stretch the other soleus.

CALF STRETCH

Use the same positioning as the soleus stretch, but position your legs further apart and straighten the back leg to stretch the calf. Stretch both calf muscles.

STRETCH AND REACH

Stand erect, with your knees slightly bent, arms overhead, and hands slightly ahead of the shoulders. Reach up with alternate arms (to stretch the abdominals).

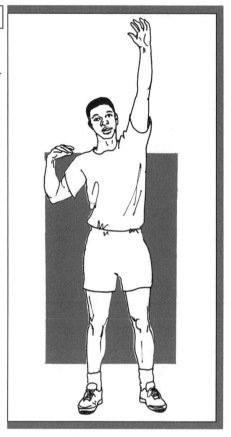

CORRECT TECHNIQUE

When you do the exercises in the following chapters, read the descriptions carefully. Use the illustrations and descriptions together to make sure you understand the proper form for each exercise. Don't rush in the early stages of your program. Start with light resistance and learn proper technique.

Take care also in moving the weight to the starting position for the various exercises using free weights. As much as possible, lift with your legs to protect your back from undue stress.

PROPER BREATHING

Don't hold your breath while performing these exercises. Doing so increases pressure within the chest cavity, which in turn causes a rapid rise in blood pressure because of the extra force put on the arteries. The rise in blood pressure diminishes the output of the heart and slows the return of the blood, via the veins, to the heart. This, in turn, leads to a rapid decrease in blood pressure. Known as the *Valsalva Maneuver*, this quick chain of events can cause dizziness, faintness, headache, and, in the extreme, short periods of blackout.

When you exercise, be sure to inhale and exhale on *every* repetition, inhaling on the preparation phase and exhaling on the effort phase. (To help out, the descriptions for the exercise with equipment in Chapters 8 and 9 describe the proper breathing patterns.) In short, simply remember this: Don't hold your breath and exhale on effort.

BACK CARE

The pelvic tilt exercise included in the routine in Chapter 6 is a good place to start when dealing with the subject of back care. Try it and get a feel for it. Its purpose is to improve strength of the gluts and abdominals and increase flexibility of the muscles in the lower back. It also conditions you to control and maintain the proper position of the pelvis and lower back.

The back has a natural, gentle curve, so it is important when exercising to avoid both excessive curvature and a back position that is too flat. Maintaining the correct curvature as you lift and move is crucial to safe and effective exercise.

HIGH-RISK EXERCISES

As our general approach is to avoid any exercise in which there is an inherent risk of injury, even when done correctly, we have purposely omitted from this book a number of common exercises. For example, those which require the body to be in a back-extension position have been excluded because they result in uneven weight-bearing on the spine and put undue stress on the lower back. Thus, supine straight-leg lifts, straight-leg sit-ups, and a number of exercises using free weights or other equipment are excluded.

We have also avoided any leg exercises which go beyond a half-squat position. More extreme, low-squat positions put excessive stress on the knee joint while also stretching the ligaments that are meant to stabilize the joint.

Overhead pressing exercises require great care. Balance is a factor, and it is crucial to maintain the proper pelvic and low-back position. Furthermore, such exercises should not be included in the early stages of a program. Exercises of a more general nature—which strengthen the trunk region and provide a solid base for these overhead lifts—should be done first.

The specific strength requirements of some sports lead competitive athletes to include some higher-risk exercises in their programs. Gymnasts and back-layout high jumpers must be strong in the back-extension position, for example, and weight lifters must do full squats. By necessity, then, they include (and usually have the strength and flexibility to handle without injury) some of the controversial exercises noted above. However, young athletes, individuals new to RT, and those conditioning for health and fitness or for recreational sports are wise to avoid them.

RATE OF PROGRESSION

Don't try for too much too soon! This is the last time we'll mention it—we promise! The "Starting" section of Chapter 4 and the "Correct Technique" section above advise you to start with light resistance and learn proper technique. "Progressing,"` in Chapter 4, explains how to modify your reps, sets, resistance, and rest interval combinations over time to provide a gradual progression. Progress at the speed your body is comfortable with, not at some predetermined rate you've set mentally.

MORE TRAINING TIPS

Wear good athletic shoes when you train—they provide traction and protection. Don't train in bare feet—even a one-kilogram plate dropped from knee height can injure an unprotected foot.

When using free weights, be sure the collars are tight and hold the plates securely on the bar. Make sure the support pin is properly in place if you're using weight-stack equipment and do all necessary adjustments to equipment—bench height, lever arm range, and so on—before you begin an exercise.

Training with a partner is also helpful, especially if you use free weights. You can help one another get the weight to the starting position and "spot" during execution of the exercise. Spotting involves being at-the-ready to help support the weight if your partner is struggling to complete the final reps in a set or to guide the movement if your partner falters or loses balance.

MOTIVATION

Somewhere between starting (the first few weeks when your program is new and exciting) and maintenance (later on when you've found your niche and you're simply maintaining what you've gained) your interest may wane and fine intentions fail. This is the time when you may have to work at sustaining your motivation. Here are some tips to help.

ROUTINE VARIATIONS

Change your routine whenever it becomes tedious or dull. If you're doing the body-weight routine in Chapter 6, try the tubing program in Chapter 7. If you're doing either of the core routines with equipment in Chapter 8, try some of the variations described. Or you can substitute exercises in the Chapter 9 catalogue for those in the core. Just remember to select exercises to ensure balanced development and arrange them to follow the work-rest principle.

You can also vary your routine by exercising at a different time of day or in a new location for a while. Return to your old routine later and it will seem new again.

TRAINING RECORD

Get in the habit of recording your progress. This will remind you when it's time to change your reps, resistance, and so on. It will also provide a tangible record of improvement which, in turn, leads to a pleasant feeling of accomplishment. (A sample Training Record chart is included at the back of the book to help you get started.)

PARTNERS

As mentioned earlier, exercising with a partner contributes to safety if you're using free weights. Furthermore, friendly challenges and good conversation can make your workout more fun. Just be sure you balance the talk and fun with sufficient work. (Actually, taking turns with a partner gives just the right rest interval between sets and exercises.) And training partners can pull each other along on days when one or the other doesn't feel quite up to it.

MUSIC

Music as a background to exercise has been called an "audio analgesic." Some people claim exercise doesn't hurt so much when there's music. Others say music takes your mind off the task at hand. Most people simply say the music makes them feel good.

If background music makes you feel good, use it. If you're doing a home routine, you can put on the tunes and get to it. If you train at a fitness facility, use of a personal cassette player will ensure that your motivating music doesn't bother others.

COMPETITION

Striving to reach reasonable goals is one way to keep your interest level high. Thoughtful program planning and a neat, accurate training record will provide an opportunity for self-competition.

You may also want to set up periodic competitions with your training partner. (Instructors can organize competitions for their class participants, and coaches can do the same with their athletes.) A Chin-up Challenge, perhaps? You decide on the competition—just be sure it's sensible and doesn't subject competitors to overexertion or risk of injury.

MOVIN' ON

We've now finished with the pre-exercise information, and it's time for some action. Consider the following, though, as you get started:

- Make sure you've completed PAR-Q. Get medical advice before you begin if PAR-Q suggests it.

- Consider the equipment and facilities at your disposal and the age/activity advisories at the beginning of Chapters 6, 7, and 8. Choose your desired routine.

- Follow the tips and advice provided for the routine you choose. Remember to warm up before each session and start with the number of sets and reps noted.

- Return to the appropriate sections here and in Chapter 4 whenever you need to refresh your memory on any of the safety or technical aspects.

6

BODY-WEIGHT EXERCISES

No equipment, you say? No problem!

Body-weight exercises—or calisthenics, as they're sometimes called—have long been used as a simple, quick method of resistance training to improve and maintain strength.

Body-weight exercises are a good place to start if you are

■ under 15 years of age;

■ an inactive, older adult (you get to decide what "older" means!); or

■ *any* age and beginning an activity program after an extended period of being sedentary.

An equipment-free routine allows you to ease gradually into resistance training before moving on to the tubing routine in Chapter 7 or the routines using weight equipment outlined in Chapter 8.

It's also a perfect maintenance program for those who usually pursue a routine with equipment, as described in Chapter 8. If you're traveling on business, away on holidays, or just too busy for a while, this exercise series (or the one in Chapter 7) can keep you going until you return to your normal routine.

For a safe, effective program, follow these guidelines:

- Warm-up first. See page 54.

- Work through the exercises leisurely the first few times you do them. Learn proper technique.

- Do them as a circuit and in the order shown. This way, you can move comfortably from one exercise to the next.

- Start with two sets of 10 repetitions of each exercise. Eliminate a few exercises initially if that proves to be too much. Add reps and sets later when you're ready for them.

- Breathe comfortably. Inhale and exhale on every repetition, exhaling on effort.

- If you are using this as a starter routine, do it for three weeks (or a minimum of nine sessions) before moving on to routines in Chapters 7 or 8.

PARTIAL CURL-UP

Starting Position: Lie supine with your legs bent and feet flat on the floor.

Movement: Press your lower back to the mat. Tighten the abdominals as you slowly curl forward, lifting your head, shoulders, and upper back off the floor. Slide your hands along the floor as you curl up. Hold the up position three to five seconds, then slowly curl back down.

Precautions: Exhale as you curl up. Keep your chin in (head in a neutral position) and look toward the ceiling, not at your knees, throughout. When doing partial curl-ups, do not anchor the feet down or use an incline board—these variations bring the hip flexors into play even more, thus decreasing the value of the curl-up for improving abdominal strength. They also put undue pressure on the lower back. Done properly, partial curl-ups ensure an appropriate balance of hip-stomach strength, which in turn contributes to proper posture.

Muscles Used:
Prime movers: abdominals
Stabilizers: hip flexors

Variations: As you feel yourself becoming stronger you can change your arm and hand positions to make the partial curl-up more challenging. Here, listed in increasing order of difficulty, are more advanced versions of the partial curl-up:

- Slide your hands up your thighs toward your knees as you curl up.

- Cross your arms on your chest throughout the movement.

- Bend your arms and place your hands against your ears throughout the movement.

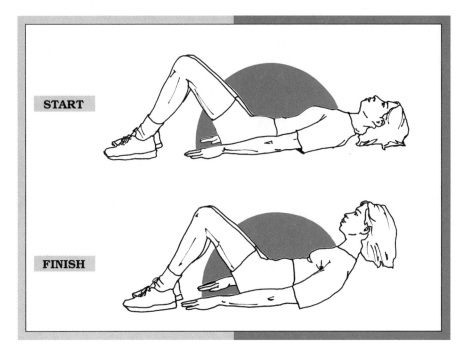

START

FINISH

PELVIC TILT

Starting Position: Lie supine with your knees bent and feet flat on the floor. Leave your arms at your sides or cross your hands on your abdominals.

Movement: Tighten your abdominals as you press your lower back and hip bones to the mat. You should feel your gluteals tighten and lift off the mat slightly.

Muscles Used:
Prime movers: abdominals and gluts

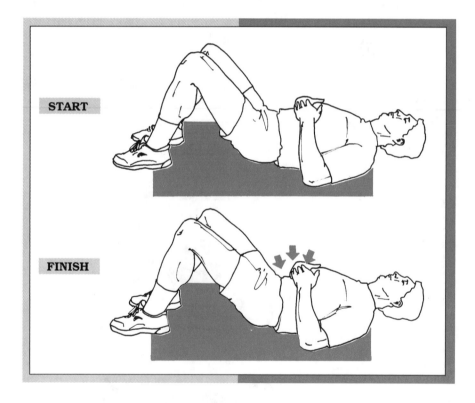

START

FINISH

CURL AND STRETCH

Starting Position: Kneel on all fours, with your knees directly under your hips and your hands under (and slightly wider than) your shoulders.

Movement: Curl one knee toward your nose, then slowly swing the leg back to a straightened, horizontal position. Return to the start position, then repeat with the opposite leg.

Precaution: Keep your head and neck neutral, looking toward the floor throughout the entire movement.

Muscles Used:
Prime movers: gluts, hamstrings, paraspinals, hip flexors, and abdominals

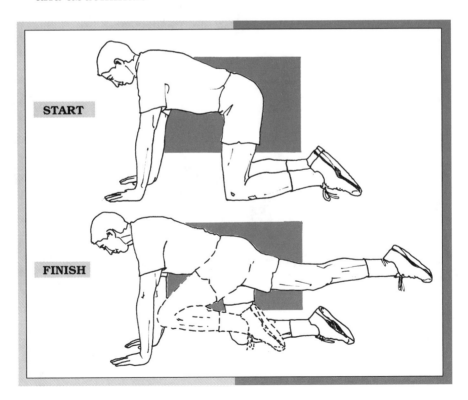

SIDE LEG RAISE

Starting Position: Lie on one side with your head resting on your forearm. Tilt your hip forward slightly.

Movement: Raise your top leg slowly. Keep the leg straight and your toes pointed toward the floor. Lower the leg and repeat. Change sides and repeat with the opposite leg.

Muscles Used:
 Prime movers: gluts and tensor fascia latae
 Stabilizers: abdominals and paraspinals

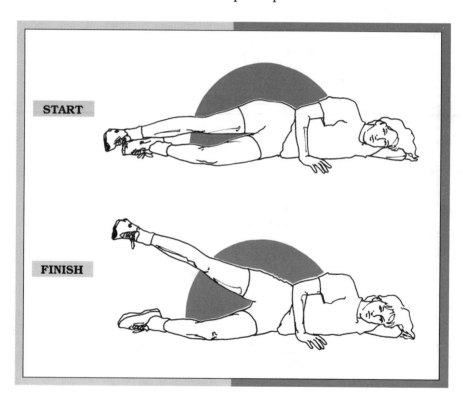

HIP TWISTER

Starting Position: Lie supine with your arms outstretched at shoulder level. Keep your head on the mat. Draw your knees toward your chest, dragging your heels on the floor.

Movement: Roll your legs to one side toward the floor while turning the head and looking toward your opposite hand. Repeat alternately to each side.

Precautions: Keep your knees together, feet on the floor, and shoulders flat on the floor throughout.

Muscles Used:
Prime movers: obliques, abdominals, and paraspinals

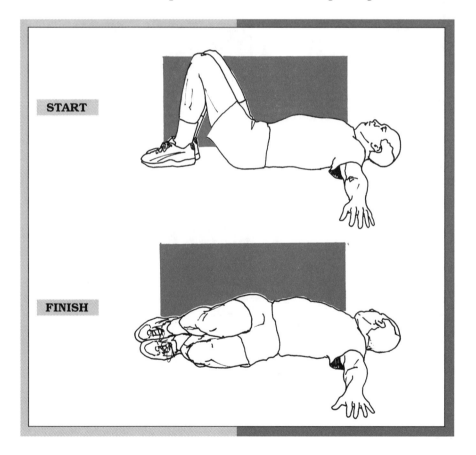

START

FINISH

SHIN PULL

Starting Position: Sit with your legs out straight.

Movement: Dorsiflex the ankles, pulling the toes toward your knees. Hold this position, pulling the toes up hard, for three to five seconds. Relax and repeat.

Muscles Used:
Prime movers: tibialis anterior

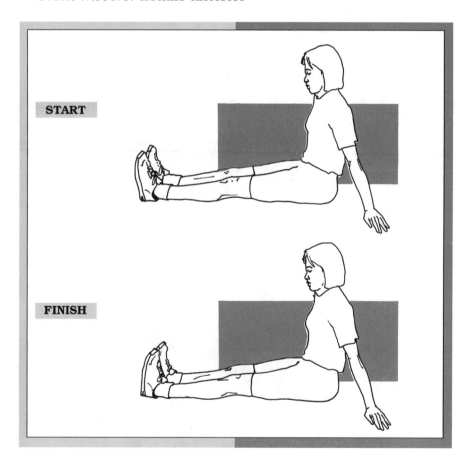

START

FINISH

STRETCH AND TUCK

Starting Position: Lie on your side with your knees slightly bent and arms outstretched overhead.

Movement: Pull your knees toward your chest. Curl your upper body and draw your arms in to arrive in a tuck position with the elbows touching your knees. Return to the starting position and repeat.

Muscles Used:
   Prime movers: abdominals, hip flexors, gluts, and paraspinals

Variation:
   ■ Do the exercise lying in a supine position, dragging your heels along the floor as you curl up.

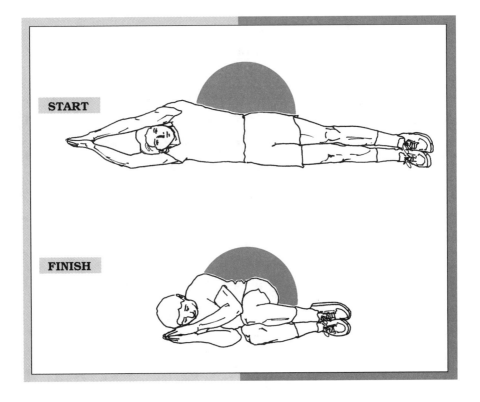

PUSH-UP

Starting Position: Lie prone with your hands at shoulder level, your palms flat on the floor slightly more than shoulder-width apart, and your toes tucked under.

Movement: Keeping your body straight, straighten your arms, exhaling, then lower your body again until it's almost touching the floor. Repeat.

Muscles Used:

Prime movers: pecs, triceps, and deltoids
Stabilizers: abdominals, paraspinals, gluts, and hip flexors

Variations:

- A less difficult push-up uses the knees rather than the feet as the pivot point.

- You can also do "incline" push-ups while standing. Lean into a wall, or place your hands on the edge of a counter or on a bench, and push up from there.

START

FINISH

ANKLE ROCKER

Starting Position: Stand with your feet three to six inches (10 to 15 cm.) apart.

Movement: Rock slowly around on the outside borders of the feet, from your heels, to one side, to your toes, to the other side. Your knees should make a small, circular motion in the same direction. Repeat in the opposite direction.

Muscles Used:

Prime movers: tibialis anterior, gastroc, soleus, and peroneus

START   FINISH

CALF RAISE

Starting Position: Stand with your feet shoulder-width apart. Keep your knees straight but not locked.

Movement: Rise up on your toes, lifting your heels as high as you can, then lower them slowly back to the floor. Repeat.

Precaution: Hold on to a chair, wall, or door frame for balance.

Muscles Used:
Prime movers: gastrocs and soleii (i.e., the soleus in each leg)

Variation:
- Do the exercise with a single leg, bending the other knee to hold your foot off the floor.

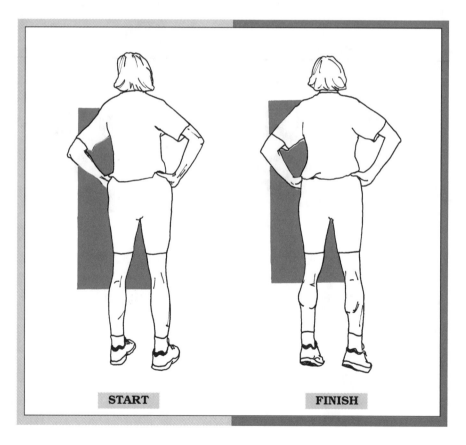

| START | FINISH |

HALF SQUAT

Starting Position: Stand with your feet shoulder-width apart and flat on the floor. Put your hands on your hips.

Movement: Squat slowly until you have a 90° bend in the knees. Straighten the legs and hips to return to the start position. Repeat.

Muscles Used:
Prime movers: quads, gluts, and hamstrings

START   FINISH

L-SEAT DIP

Starting Position: Place two sturdy chairs shoulder-width apart. Support yourself with your palms on the chairs and your arms straight. Place your legs in front, knees straight and heels on the floor.

Movement: Lower the body toward the floor by bending the elbows. Straighten the arms returning to the start position. Repeat.

Precaution: Go down only as far as is comfortable for you. You can go lower as you get stronger.

Muscles Used:
Prime movers: pecs, triceps, and lats
Stabilizers: deltoids

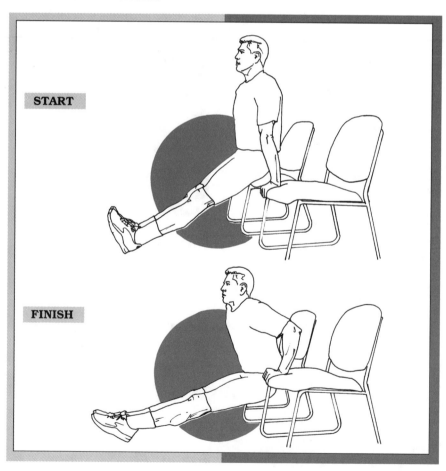

START

FINISH

7

TUBING
EXERCISES

Tubing is a great resistance training routine for anyone. It's a particularly excellent place to start if you are

■ under 15 years of age;

■ a reasonably active older adult just getting started with resistance training; or

■ *any* age and becoming active again after an extended period of time being sedentary.

This is an ideal routine if you want to go beyond the body-weight exercises in Chapter 6 but don't have access to the free weights or stack weights needed for the routines in Chapter 8. (See Chapter 4, page 47 for information on the cost and availability of tubing.)

Along with body-weight exercises, tubing exercises can keep you going if you're traveling for business or pleasure or you just want a break from a routine using weights.

Tubing provides a versatile RT program. With the examples included here and a little thought and planning, most—if not all—of the exercises in the next two chapters can be performed with tubing. Here are three hints for safe and efficient routines:

- **Handles are handy.** If you have a tubing kit with handles attached, you're all set. If you have a simple length of tubing (a 12-foot piece is recommended), you should tie a loop at each end large enough to fit your hand comfortably.

- **Anchor for exercise.** For many exercises, you anchor the tubing by standing on it or holding it with your hand. For some, however, it is most efficient to have an anchoring point away from your body. Attaching a sturdy loop of nylon webbing or other similar material allows you to tie the tubing to various immovable objects such as a bed leg or couch, or a sturdy hook on the wall. The loop will help prevent nicks and cuts in your tubing which might occur from attaching it directly to other objects. (Tubing is very durable, but you should check it regularly for nicks, cuts, or weak spots, so there is no risk of it snapping when in use.)

- **Adjust for length and resistance.** The shorter the length of tubing you stretch, the greater the resistance. If an exercise is too easy, shorten the length between your hand, foot, or leg and the anchoring point. (If you're using an anchoring point away from your body, you can move further away from it to accomplish the same thing.) To reduce the resistance do the opposite. The further you stretch the tubing, the more resistance you get, and the longer the length of tubing that you are stretching, the more gradual the increase in resistance. You can also increase the resistance by doubling the tubing. You'll have to experiment the first few times you do the exercises to determine the right combination of length and resistance. Be sure to go through the entire range of motion required for each exercise.

Here are a few more tubing tips:

- Warm up first. See page 54.

- Don't rush. Learn proper technique.

- Do the routine as a circuit in the order shown. Start with two sets of 10 repetitions of each exercise.

- Inhale and exhale on every repetition, exhaling on effort.

- Anchor the tubing securely (to yourself or an external anchor point), maintain proper body positions, and perform the exercises correctly.

- If you use this as a starter routine, do it for three weeks (or a minimum of nine sessions) before moving on to either of the routines in Chapter 8.

CHEST PRESS

Starting Position: Lie supine, legs bent, feet flat on the floor, and shortened tubing under your shoulders. Place elbows on the floor at chest height and hands above the elbows, using a pronated grip.

Movement: Press to arm's length, exhaling. Return slowly to the start position, inhaling.

Muscles Used:
   Prime movers: pecs, triceps, and deltoids

Variation:

■ This exercise can also be performed seated in a chair with the center of the tubing anchored directly behind you and the tubing lightly stretched and at chest height. Bend elbows at chest height, with hands a little more than shoulder-width apart and held at chest height in a pronated grip. Press to arm's length, exhaling. Return slowly to the start position, inhaling.

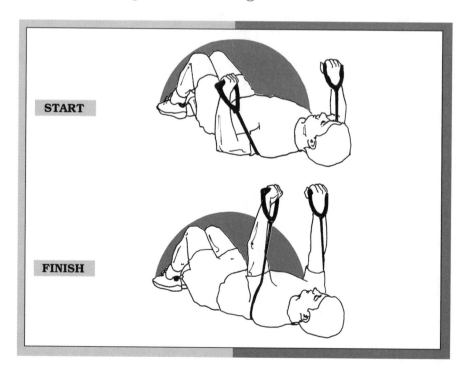

START

FINISH

Half Squat

Starting Position: Stand on the center of the tubing with your feet shoulder-width apart and your arms straight at your sides, with the tubing in a fully stretched position. Look straight ahead, abdominals tight and chest up.

Movement: Slowly squat until you attain a 90° bend at the knee. Inhale as you squat. Return to the start position, exhaling.

Muscles Used:
Prime movers: quads, gluts, and hamstrings
Stabilizers: abdominals and paraspinals

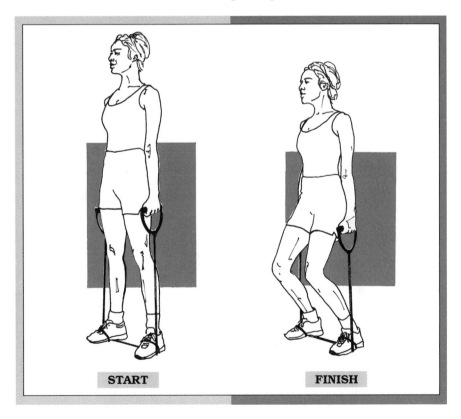

START   FINISH

BENT-OVER ONE-ARM ROW

Starting Position: Lean on a chair or bench with one arm, knees slightly bent, hips bent, and back nearly parallel to the floor. Stand on the tubing with one foot, the other foot slightly behind for stability. Hold the tubing in your free hand, letting your arm hang straight down from your shoulder, keeping the tubing lightly stretched.

Movement: Keep your elbow close to your body and inhale as you pull your hand up to the front of your shoulder. Lower to the start position, exhaling. Repeat, then change arms.

Muscles Used:
Prime movers: biceps, lats, trapezius, teres major, rhomboids, and deltoids

Variations:

- Position yourself as above but with one knee kneeling on the bench or chair as well (i.e., left hand and knee on bench).

- Sit with the center of the tubing anchored in front of you at chest height and use both arms at once. For stability, you can sit facing backward on a chair and lean on the chair back to reduce strain on the lower back.

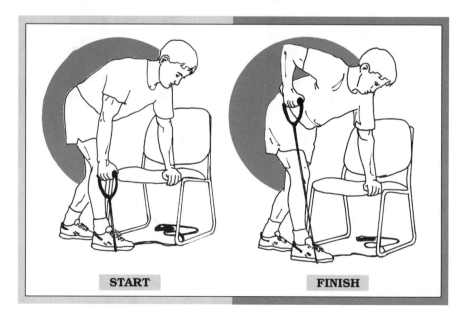

START   FINISH

PARTIAL CURL-UP

Note: You will not use tubing for this exercise. We have included it in the tubing program because abdominal muscles are important for trunk stabilization in almost every physical activity.

Starting Position: Lie supine with your legs bent and feet flat on the floor.

Movement: Press your lower back to the mat. Tighten the abdominals as you slowly curl forward, lifting your head, shoulders, and upper back off the floor. Slide your hands along the floor as you curl up. Hold the up position three to five seconds, then slowly curl back down.

Precautions: Breathe out as you curl up. Keep your chin in (head in a neutral position) and look toward the ceiling, not at your knees, throughout. When doing partial curl-ups do not anchor the feet down or use an incline board; these variations bring the hip flexors into play even more, thus decreasing the value of the curl-up for improving abdominal strength. They also put undue pressure on the lower back. Done properly, partial curl-ups ensure an appropriate balance of hip-stomach strength, which in turn contributes to proper posture.

Muscles Used:
Prime movers: abdominals
Stabilizers: hip flexors

Variations: As you feel yourself becoming stronger, you can change your arm and hand positions to make the partial curl-up more challenging. Here, listed in increasing order of difficulty, are more advanced versions of the partial curl-up:

■ Slide your hands up your thighs toward your knees as you curl up.

■ Cross your arms on your chest throughout the movement.

■ Bend your arms and place your hands against your ears throughout the movement.

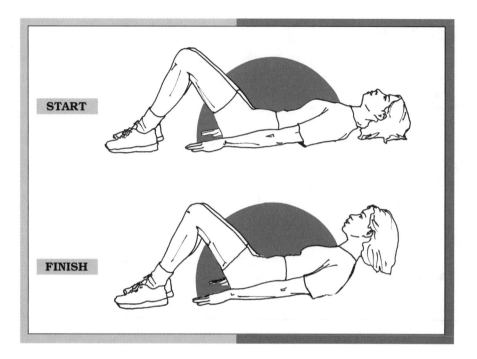

START

FINISH

BICEPS CURL

Starting Position: Stand with your back straight, arms straight at your sides, holding lightly stretched tubing in a supinated grip.

Movement: Curl your hands to shoulder height, exhaling. Inhale as you lower the hands to the start position.

Precaution: Keep your elbows at your sides and maintain a slight knee bend throughout the movement.

Muscles Used:
Prime movers: biceps and brachialis

Variations:

■ Do the exercise one arm at a time.

■ Do the exercise in a seated position.

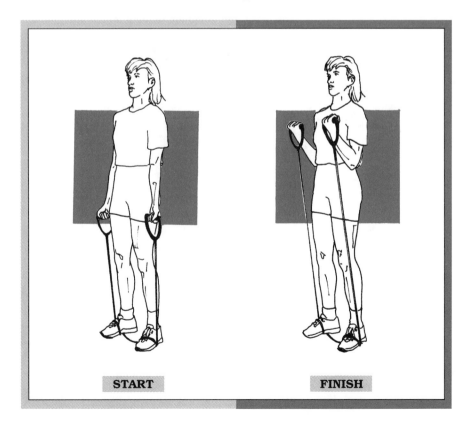

| START | FINISH |

TRICEPS PRESS

Starting Position: Stand (or sit) and anchor the tubing at your left shoulder with your left hand. Hold the handle of the tubing with the right hand, elbow out to the side at shoulder height and bent, with the tubing lightly stretched.

Movement: Press your right hand out to the side, straightening the elbow. Keep the elbow and hand at shoulder height and exhale as you press out. Repeat, then change arms.

Muscles Used:
  Prime movers: triceps
  Stabilizers: deltoids and traps

Variation:

  ■ Triceps Pressdown: Position as above, but keep the elbow at your side and press down.

START   FINISH

SEATED CALF PRESS (SINGLE LEG)

Starting Position: Sit on the floor (or on a chair) with the center of the tubing looped around the arch of one foot. Straighten the leg, keeping the opposite knee bent and foot flat on the floor. Hold the tubing, lightly stretched, in both hands at the chest.

Movement: Keep the leg straight as you plantar flex (point the toe down) as far as you can. Repeat, then change legs.

Muscles Used:
Prime movers: gastrocs and soleii

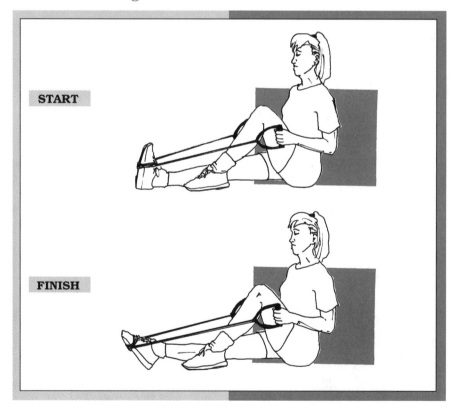

START

FINISH

SHOULDER (UPRIGHT) ROW

Starting Position: Stand on the center of the tubing with your feet shoulder-width apart, your back straight, and a slight bend in the knees. Hold the tubing, lightly stretched, in each hand with the arms straight and hanging down in front.

Movement: Keeping the hands close to your body and your elbows above your hands at all times, pull your hands up to chest level, inhaling. Return slowly to the start position, exhaling.

Precaution: Lift the arms only as high as mid-chest (i.e., nipple) level.

Muscles Used:
Prime movers: deltoids, trapezius, biceps, and brachialis
Stabilizers: paraspinals and abdominals

Variation:
■ As above, but grasp the opposite tube/handle so that the tubing and your arms are crossed in front of you.

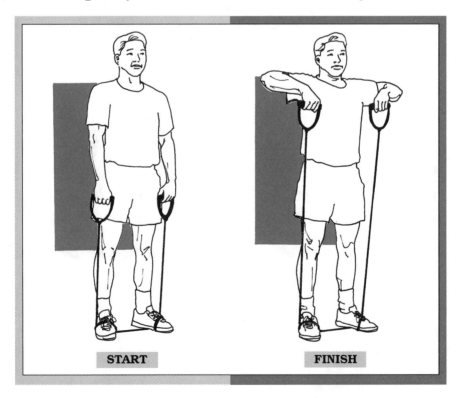

START   FINISH

SEATED HIP ABDUCTION

Starting Position: Sit on the floor and loop the tubing around your leg just below the knee. Bend your other leg and anchor the opposite end of the tubing by passing it under your other foot and holding it with your hand.

Movement: Keep your toes and knee pointed up as you slide your leg to the side as far as you can, exhaling. Return to the start position, inhaling. Repeat, then change legs.

Muscles Used:
Prime movers: gluts and tensor fascia latae

Variation:

■ Lying on your side, do side-leg raise as in Chapter 6 (page 72). Secure tubing just below both knees (bottom leg serving as the anchor).

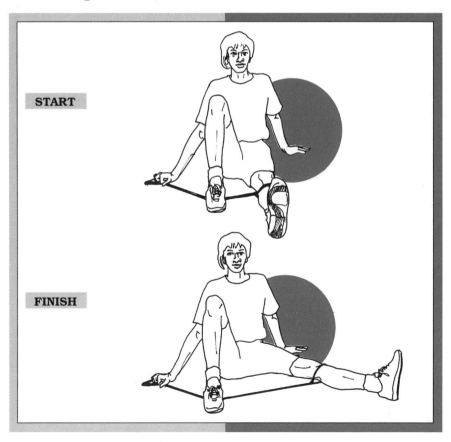

START

FINISH

SEATED HIP ADDUCTION

Starting Position: Sit on the floor and loop the tubing around your leg just below the knee. Anchor the opposite end of the tubing to a fixed object opposite to your knee. Start with your leg abducted and the tubing lightly stretched.

Movement: Keep your toes and knee pointed up as you slide your leg toward your opposite leg as far as you can, exhaling. Return to the start position, inhaling. Repeat, then change legs.

Muscles Used:
Prime movers: hip adductors

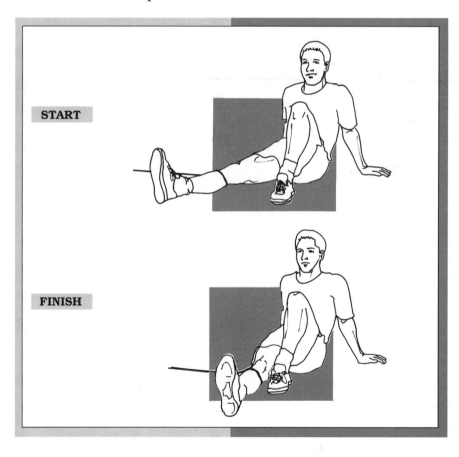

START

FINISH

8

WEIGHT
TRAINING
EXERCISES

This chapter provides two different routines: one using free weights and one using stack-weight equipment. Each routine includes ten exercises and provides an overall, balanced program. The routine you choose will depend on where you will be doing your training sessions and the equipment you will have available.

RT with free weights or stack weights is a good place to start if you are

■ a reasonably fit adult adding resistance training to your activity routine;

- an active adult wishing to do some basic conditioning for a recreational activity; or

- an athlete just getting started with resistance training for a sport.

The exercise descriptions and accompanying illustrations provide everything you need to understand the exercises and execute them safely. Read the description the first few times you do each exercise; after that, a quick look at the illustration under the heading of the exercise will likely be enough to remind you what you're supposed to do. Please note the following:

- Many exercises are known by more than one name, but in the chapters that follow we use only the simplest and most common. In almost every case, the name indicates the body part or muscle group exercised and the action performed; hence, chest press, biceps curl, and so on.

- For exercises using weight-stack equipment (in this chapter and in Chapter 9), the "station" where each exercise is performed is listed. Look for a wall poster depicting the stations on the equipment in your training facility and seek help from an instructor if there is nothing posted to identify the various stations or equipment.

Final Tips and Reminders

- Refer to Chapter 4 to determine your starting sets, reps, resistance, and rest interval. (See the Program Design Summary on page 46.)

- Use a continuous, controlled (not too fast, not too slow) movement. Don't pause between repetitions and don't "bang" the weights down when returning to the starting position.

- Strive for a correct body position, maintain your balance, and keep your abdominal muscles tight to help stabilize the lower back.

- For exercises done in a standing position, keep your feet shoulder-width apart unless noted otherwise.

- The chest press needn't always be your first exercise. Start with whichever you like, just be sure to do them in the order they are listed.

- If an exercise feels uncomfortable, get someone with RT experience to watch you and correct your technique. If it continues to feel uncomfortable even when performed correctly, substitute another exercise for it for the time being. Return to it later and try it again.

- Do your core routine for five weeks (or a minimum of 10 to 15 sessions) before trying any of the variations noted here or substituting exercises from the Chapter 9 catalogue.

- For exercises done lying supine on a bench, keep the back of your head, your back, and your buttocks flat on the bench and your feet flat on the floor throughout the movement. If it helps to keep your back flat on the bench, you can place your feet on a low bench or box.

CORE ROUTINE USING FREE WEIGHTS

CHEST PRESS

Starting Position: Lie supine on a bench, feet raised and flat on a small box. Use a pronated grip on a barbell, with hands slightly more than shoulder-width apart.

Movement: Lower the weight slowly to the chest (to the start position), inhaling; press the bar back to arm's length, exhaling. No pause between repetitions.

Precautions: Make sure your head, back, and buttocks remain in contact with the bench throughout the movement. (Your knees should be slightly higher than your hips to minimize the pressure on the lower back.) Avoid extremely wide grips, as they place undue stress on the shoulder joints.

Muscles Used:
Prime movers: pecs, triceps, and deltoids

Variations:

- Use dumbbells instead of a barbell.

- Vary your grip width. A wider grip works the pecs more, a narrower grip works the triceps more.

START

FINISH

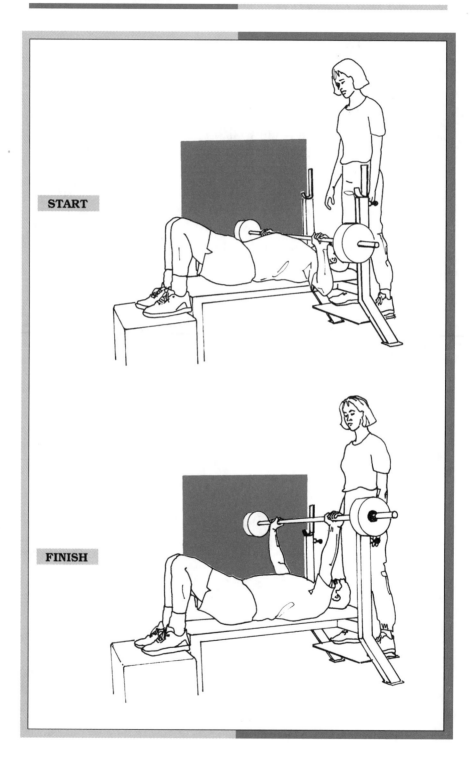

HALF SQUAT

Starting Position: Stand with your knees slightly bent, back straight, and head up. Hold the barbell on your shoulders, securing it with a pronated grip.

Movement: Look straight ahead, abdominals tight and chest up, and slowly squat until you attain a 90° bend at the knee, inhaling as you squat. Return to starting position, exhaling.

Precautions: Have someone assist in placing the barbell on your shoulders, passing it to you from behind. This person could also watch to ensure you don't go beyond a 90° bend at the knee. For extra safety, do the exercise over a bench or chair—you can sit down on it if you can't complete a repetition or if you lose your balance.

Muscles Used:
Prime movers: quads and gluts
Assistant movers: hamstrings
Stabilizers: paraspinals, abdominals, and adductors

Variations:

- Hold dumbbells in each hand and with the arms at the sides instead of a barbell on the shoulders.

- Perform a quarter squat using heavier weights.

START

FINISH

BENT-OVER SHOULDER ROW

Starting Position: Lean on a bench with one arm, knees slightly bent, hips bent, back parallel to the floor. Hold a dumbbell in your free hand, letting your arm hang straight down from your shoulder.

Movement: Keep your elbow close to your body and inhale as you pull the dumbbell up to the front of your shoulder. Lower to the start position, exhaling. Repeat, then change arms.

Muscles Used:
Prime movers: biceps, lats, teres major, and rhomboids
Stabilizers: trapezius, deltoids, pecs, and others

Variations:

■ Position yourself as above but with one knee kneeling on the bench as well (i.e., right arm and leg on bench).

■ Lie on a high bench and use both arms at once.

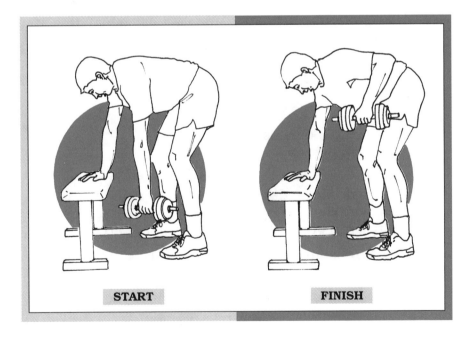

START FINISH

PARTIAL CURL-UP

Note: You will not use free weights for this exercise. We have included it in this program because abdominal muscles are important for trunk stabilization in almost every physical activity.

Starting Position: Lie supine with your legs bent and feet flat on the floor.

Movement: Press your lower back to the mat. Tighten the abdominals as you slowly curl forward, lifting your head, shoulders, and upper back off the floor. Slide your hands along the floor as you curl up. Hold the up position three to five seconds, then slowly curl back down.

Precautions: Exhale as you curl up. Keep your chin in (head in a neutral position) and look toward the ceiling, not at your knees, throughout. When doing partial curl-ups, do not anchor the feet down or use an incline board; these variations bring the hip flexors into play even more, thus decreasing the value of the curl-up for improving abdominal strength. They also put undue pressure on the lower back. Done properly, partial curl-ups ensure an appropriate balance of hip-stomach strength, which in turn contributes to proper posture.

Muscles Used:
Prime movers: abdominals
Stabilizers: hip flexors

Variations: As you feel yourself becoming stronger you can change your arm and hand positions to make the partial curl-up more challenging. Here, listed in increasing order of difficulty, are more advanced versions of the partial curl-up:

■ Slide your hands up your thighs toward your knees as you curl up.

■ Cross your arms on your chest throughout the movement.

■ Bend your arms and place your hands against your ears throughout the movement.

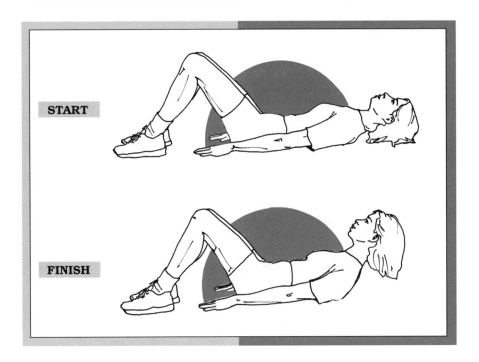

START

FINISH

BICEPS CURL

Starting Position: Stand with your back straight and head up. Hold a barbell with a supinated grip, your arms straight and hands shoulder-width apart.

Movement: Curl the bar to shoulder height, exhaling. Inhale as you lower the bar to the starting position. Keep your elbows at your sides and maintain a slight bend in the knees throughout the movement.

Muscles Used:
Prime movers: biceps and brachialis

Variations:

- Reverse Biceps Curl—same position/movement as above, but with a pronated grip. This uses the wrist extensors and brachioradialis more.

- Use dumbbells (alternating or together) instead of a barbell.

START   FINISH

TRICEPS PRESS

Starting Position: Lie supine on a bench with your feet flat on the floor. Hold a barbell at arm's length directly above the shoulders. Use a pronated grip, with your hands shoulder-width apart.

Movement: Keeping the elbows in position directly above the shoulders, lower the bar by bending your elbows until it nearly reaches your forehead, inhaling. Press the bar back to the starting position, exhaling.

Precaution: Your elbows should remain at shoulder-width and stationary throughout the motion.

Muscles Used:

Prime movers: triceps

Stabilizers: deltoids, pecs, and lats

Variations:

- Use the same body position, but with a supinated grip.
- Use dumbbells instead of a barbell.

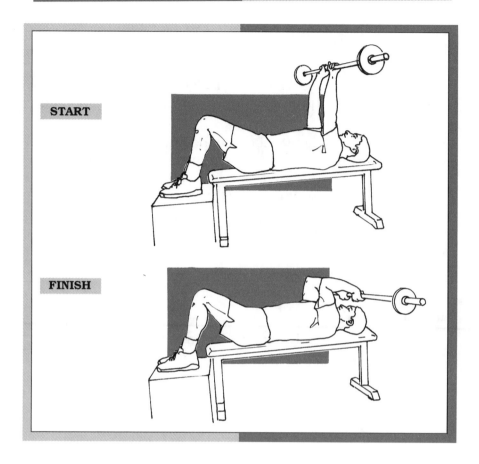

START

FINISH

CALF RAISE

Starting Position: Stand with your back straight and head up. Hold a barbell on your shoulders, securing it with a pronated grip.

Movement: Keeping your legs straight, raise up on your toes as far as possible, exhaling as you do so. Lower slowly to the starting position, inhaling as you return your heels to the floor.

Precaution: Have someone assist in placing a barbell on your shoulders, passing it to you from behind. Have them help lift it off as well.

Muscles Used:
Prime movers: gastrocs and soleii
Assistant movers: peroneus

Variations:

■ For greater range of motion, raise the balls of the feet on a block. For safety, start with a one-inch block, then progress to a two-inch block later. Remember to lower your heels slowly.

■ Single-Leg Calf Raise—hold a dumbbell in one hand, with the other hand on a chair or against a wall for balance.

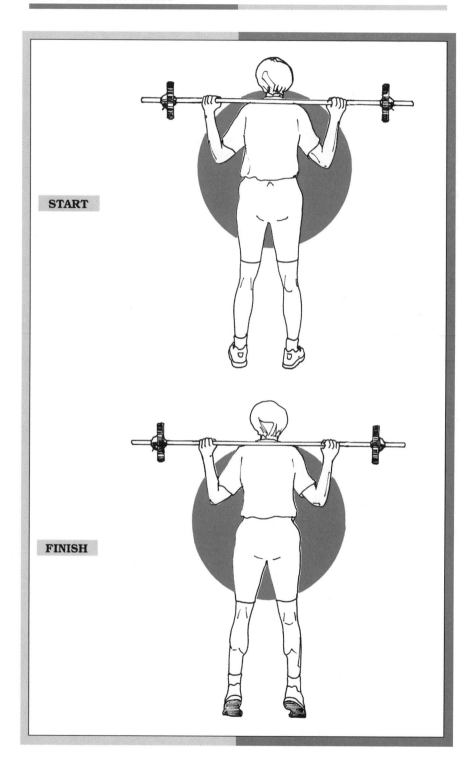

START

FINISH

SHOULDER (UPRIGHT) ROW

Starting Position: Stand with your back straight, head up, and a slight bend in the knees. Hold a barbell (with your hands placed 8 to 12 inches apart in the center of the bar) with a pronated grip, letting the bar hang in front at arm's length.

Movement: Keeping the bar close to your body and your elbows above the bar at all times, pull the bar up to chest level, inhaling. Return the bar slowly to the starting position, exhaling.

Precaution: Lift the bar only as high as mid-chest (i.e., nipple) level.

Muscles Used:
Prime movers: deltoids, traps, biceps, and brachialis

Variation:

■ Use dumbbells instead of a barbell.

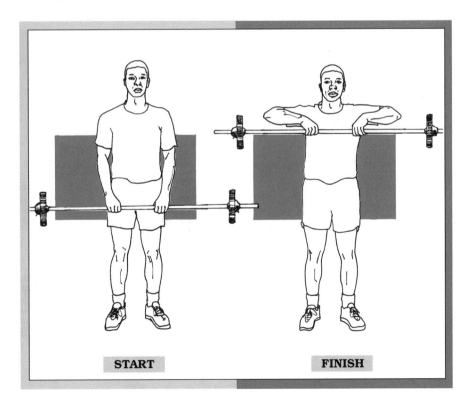

START   FINISH

HIP ABDUCTION

Starting Position: Strap a Velcro/soft weight around one leg (just below the knee). Lie on your side with the weighted leg on top and your head supported on your bottom arm. Bend the knee of your bottom leg, but keep your top leg straight. Place the hand of your top arm on the floor in front of your abdominals and lean your hip slightly forward.

Movement: Keep your toes and knee pointed forward as you lift your top leg, exhaling. Return to the start position, inhaling. Repeat, then change legs.

Muscles Used:
  Prime movers: gluts and tensor fascia latae
  Stabilizers: paraspinals, abdominals, and hip flexors

Variation:

  ■ This exercise can also be performed without weight.

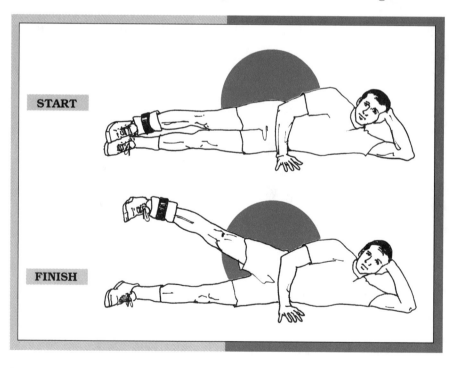

START

FINISH

HIP ADDUCTION

Starting Position: Strap a Velcro/soft weight around the leg (just below the knee). Lie on your side with the weighted leg on the bottom and your head supported on your bottom arm. Keep the bottom leg straight. Bend the top leg at the knee and hip and place your foot in front of the knee of the bottom leg. Keep one hip above the other (i.e., don't lean the pelvis forward or backward).

Movement: Keep the toe and knee pointed forward as you lift your bottom leg, exhaling. Return to the start position, inhaling. Repeat, then change legs.

Muscles Used:
Prime movers: hip adductors
Stabilizers: paraspinals, abdominals, and hip flexors

Variation:

■ This exercise can also be performed without weight.

CORE ROUTINE USING WEIGHT-STACK EQUIPMENT

CHEST PRESS

Station: Chest-Press

Starting Position: Lie supine on a bench with your feet flat on a small box, shoulder-width apart. Use a pronated grip on the bar, hands slightly more than shoulder-width apart.

Movement: Inhale, then press the bar to arm's length, exhaling. Lower the bar slowly, inhaling. Don't pause with your arms straight or set the weight down between reps.

Precautions: Make sure your head, back, and buttocks remain in contact with the bench throughout the movement. (Your knees should be slightly higher than your hips to minimize the pressure on your lower back.) Avoid extremely wide grips, as they place undue stress on the shoulder joint.

Muscles Used:
Prime movers: pecs, triceps, and deltoids

Variation:

■ Use different grip widths. A wider grip works the pecs more, a narrower grip works the triceps more.

START   FINISH

LEG PRESS

Station: Leg-Press

Starting Position: Sit with your back flat against the back of the chair. Set the seat to provide a 90° bend (no more) at the knee and place your feet (insteps) on the pedals. For balance and support, grasp the handles on both sides of the chair.

Movement: Straighten your legs, pushing the foot pedals away from you, exhaling. Return slowly to the starting position, inhaling. Don't lock the knees (keep a slight bend in them) in the straightened position.

Muscles Used:
Prime movers: quads, gluts, and hamstrings
Stabilizers: paraspinals

Variation:

■ Some weight-stack equipment has a second set of foot pedals above the lower set. The load is greater using the top pedals (see the amount marked on the weight stack) and the gluts and hamstrings are exercised more.

START

FINISH

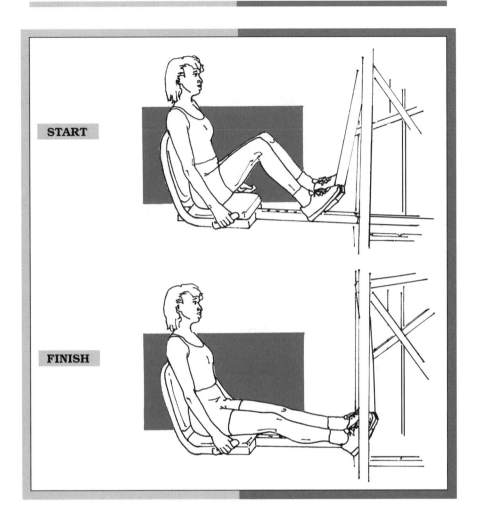

LAT PULLDOWN

Station: High-Pulley with Lat Bar

Starting Position: Take a supinated grip on the bar with hands slightly more than shoulder-width apart. Kneel on one knee with your back straight and your arms extended so that your head is slightly in front of the upper pulley wheel.

Movement: Inhale, then pull the bar down in front of your head to shoulder level with a smooth arm and shoulder action while exhaling. Return the bar slowly to the starting position, inhaling.

Precautions: Keep your abdominals tight and avoid leaning back as you pull the bar down.

Muscles Used:
Prime movers: lats and biceps
Assistant movers: traps and rhomboids
Stabilizers: deltoids

Variation:

- Use a pronated grip with the hands (comfortably) more than shoulder-width apart and pull the bar down in front of your body. (Avoid pulling the bar down behind the head with a wide pronated grip, as this places excessive stress on the shoulder joint.)

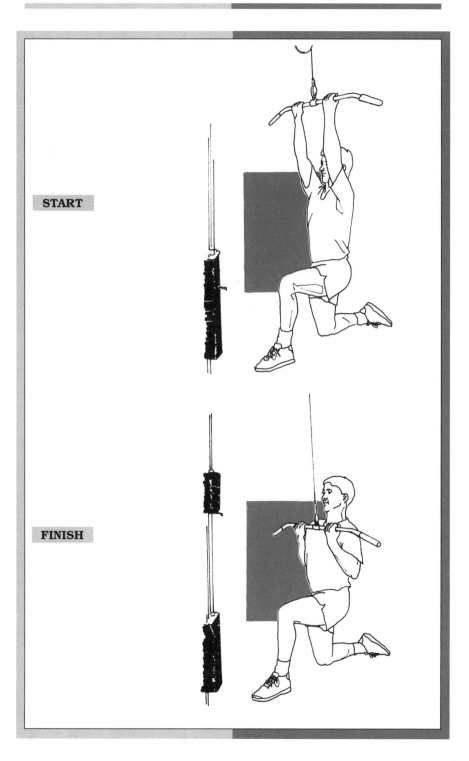

START

FINISH

PARTIAL CURL-UP

Note: We have included this exercise in the weight-stack program because abdominal muscles are important for trunk stabilization in almost every physical activity.

Station: Do this exercise on a mat on the floor, using no external equipment. Do not use the sit-up/curl-up station if there is one.

Starting Position: Lie supine with your legs bent and feet flat on the floor.

Movement: Press your lower back to the mat. Tighten the abdominals as you slowly curl forward, lifting your head, shoulders, and upper back off the floor. Slide your hands along the floor as you curl up. Hold the up position three to five seconds, then slowly curl back down.

Precautions: Exhale as you curl up. Keep your chin in (head in a neutral position) and look toward the ceiling, not at your knees, throughout. When doing partial curl-ups, do not anchor the feet down or use an incline board; these variations bring the hip flexors into play even more, thus decreasing the value of the curl-up for improving abdominal strength. They also put undue pressure on the lower back. Done properly, partial curl-ups ensure an appropriate balance of hip-stomach strength, which in turn contributes to proper posture.

Muscles Used:
Prime movers: abdominals
Stabilizers: hip flexors

Variations: As you feel yourself becoming stronger you can change your arm and hand positions to make the partial curl-up more challenging. Here, listed in increasing order of difficulty, are more advanced versions of the partial curl-up:

- Slide your hands up your thighs toward your knees as you curl up.

- Cross your arms on your chest throughout the movement.

- Bend your arms and place your hands against your ears throughout the movement.

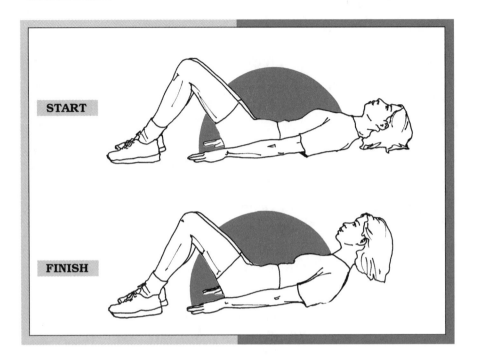

START

FINISH

BICEPS CURL

Station: Low-Pulley with Short Bar

Starting Position: Stand with your back and arms straight, using a supinated grip on the bar with hands shoulder-width apart.

Movement: Inhale, then curl the bar to shoulder height, exhaling. Lower the bar to the starting position slowly while inhaling.

Precaution: Keep your head up, your elbows at your sides, and your knees slightly bent throughout the movement.

Muscles Used:
Prime movers: biceps and brachialis

Variation:

- Reverse Biceps Curl—use the same position and movement as above, but with a pronated grip. This position uses the wrist extensors more.

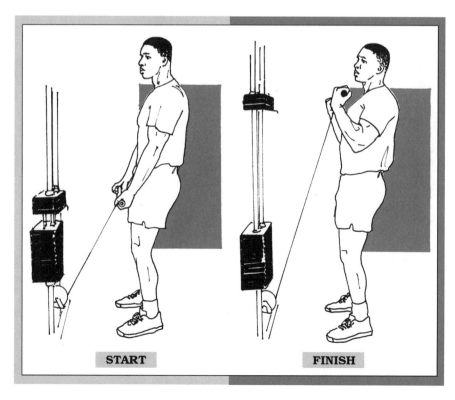

START   FINISH

TRICEPS PRESSDOWN

Station: High-Pulley. Use an inverted U-handle if one is available. Otherwise, a straight bar is fine.

Starting Position: Stand close to the bar with one foot in front of the other and leaning slightly forward from the hip. Keeping your back straight and your elbows close to your sides, take a pronated grip on the bar with the hands close together at the center of the bar.

Movement: Start with the elbows bent at 90°, inhale, then push your hands down until your arms are straight, exhaling. Return to the starting position slowly while inhaling. Keep your elbows at your sides, your knees slightly bent, and your shoulders down throughout the movement.

Muscles Used:
Prime movers: triceps
Stabilizers: lats and pecs

START

FINISH

CALF PRESS

Station: Leg-Press

Starting Position: Sit as for leg press (with the seat positioned as far back as possible), with your feet parallel and shoulder-width apart. Place the balls of the feet just above the bottom edge of the lower footrests. Straighten your legs but don't lock your knees, and dorsiflex your ankles (i.e., pull your toes toward you).

Movement: Plantarflex your ankles (i.e., press the balls of your feet away from you.) Then dorsiflex your ankles again, slowly returning to the starting position. Keep your legs straight and breathe normally throughout the movement.

Precaution: Use considerably less weight for this exercise than you do for the leg press.

Muscles Used:
Prime movers: gastrocs and soleii
Assistant movers: peroneus

Variations:

■ Do one leg at a time

■ Use the shoulder-press station and the same action as for the calf raise with a barbell.

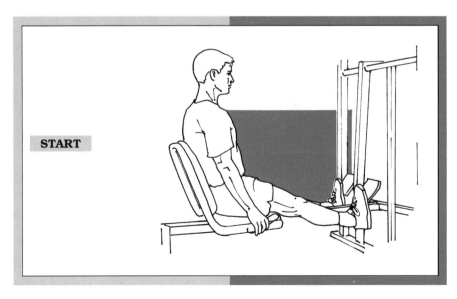

START

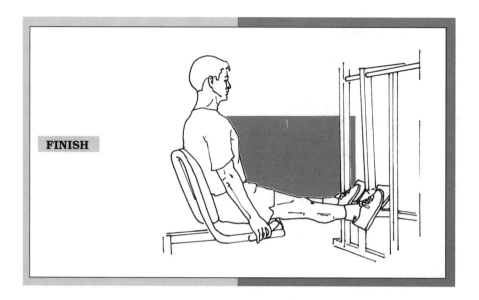

FINISH

SEATED SHOULDER ROW

Station: Low-Pulley with a short, straight bar or a close-grip double handle.

Starting Position: Sit on the floor facing the pulley station with your knees slightly bent and feet braced. Take a supinated grip on the bar with the hands about shoulder-width apart and bend slightly forward from the waist.

Movement: Pull the bar to your chest, inhaling. Return to the starting position, exhaling. Keep your shoulders down (not "hunched") throughout the movement.

Precaution: You should lean back slightly as you pull back.

Muscles Used:
Prime movers: lats and biceps
Assistant movers: deltoids, teres, traps, and rhomboids
Stabilizers: paraspinals

Variation:

- Use the same position and movement, but with a pronated grip. This variation works the biceps more.

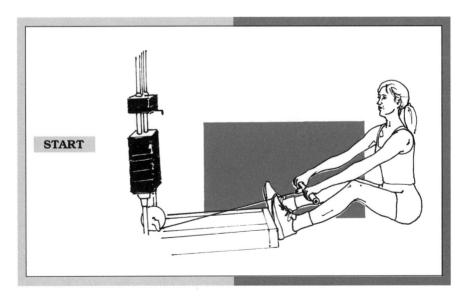

START

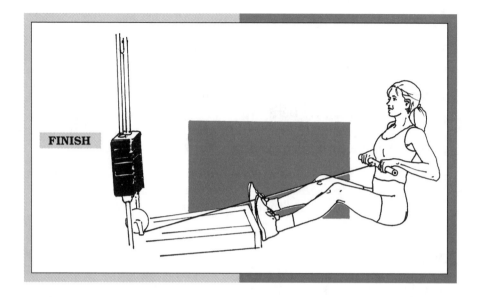

FINISH

HIP ABDUCTION

Station: Low-Pulley using a padded strap with a D-ring attachment.

Starting Position: Stand sideways and at arm's length from the pulley station, with the padded loop placed just below the knee of the leg farthest from the machine. Start with this leg crossed in front of your support leg so that your knee is at the mid-line of your body.

Movement: With your near arm braced against the machine, pull the leg away from the machine while exhaling. Return slowly to the starting position, inhaling. Keep your abdominals tight and your hips level and stationary throughout the movement. Repeat with the other leg.

Muscles Used:
Prime movers: gluts
Assistant movers: tensor fascia latae
Stabilizers: hip abductors and adductors (support leg), abdominals, and paraspinals

Variation:
■ This exercise can also be done seated on the floor facing sideways to the pulley station so that your knee is directly in front of the pulley. Bend the near (uninvolved) leg so that the pulley cable passes under it.

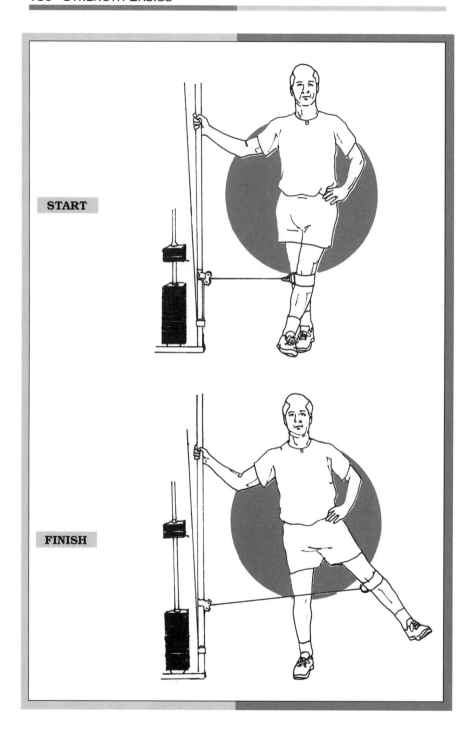

START

FINISH

HIP ADDUCTION

Station: Low-Pulley using a padded strap with a D-ring attachment.

Starting Position: Stand sideways and at arm's length from the pulley station with the padded loop placed just below the knee of the leg nearest the machine.

Movement: With your near arm straight and braced against the machine, pull the leg across in front of you, exhaling. Return slowly to the starting position, inhaling. Keep your abdominals tight and your hips level and stationary throughout the movement. Repeat with the other leg.

Muscles Used:
Prime movers: hip adductors
Stabilizers: hip abductors and adductors (support leg), abdominals, paraspinals

Variation:

- ▪ This exercise can also be done seated on the floor facing sideways to the pulley station so that your knee is directly in front of the pulley. Abduct the far (uninvolved) leg so that the near leg has a greater range of motion and can cross the mid-line of your body.

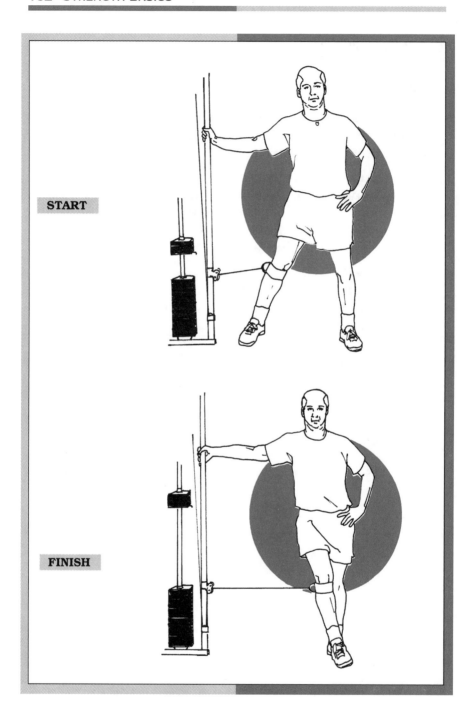

START

FINISH

9

MORE
EXERCISES

Either one of Chapter 8's core routines will get you off to a solid start with RT using equipment. However, if you do the same thing for too long, your routine may start to feel like a rut. The exercises in this chapter are intended to offer variety and choices that allow you to alter your program to keep it interesting and challenging.

Remember that you should stick to your core routine for five weeks (or a minimum of 10 to 15 sessions). After that, you can use the exercises outlined here as substitutes for those in the core, for the sake of variety, or to add to the core to increase the demands of your program.

If you're substituting, be sure to check the "Muscles Used" descriptions to ensure you do so correctly. If you're adding exercises, do so gradually (one per week to a maximum of 15 or 16). You may also want to break up your circuit into groups of exercises or minicircuits, as described in Chapter 4.

The exercises in this chapter use free weights, weight-stack type equipment, and tubing. Where more than one type of equipment can be used, the main description and illustration refer to only one type; other equipment options are described in "Variations." The movement, precautions, and so on will be the same regardless of the equipment used.

ARM LATERAL RAISE

Starting Position: Stand with your back straight and a slight bend at your knees and hips. With your arms extended, but elbows slightly bent, hold dumbbells at your sides with the palms facing in.

Movement: Keeping your elbows slightly bent and palms facing down, raise your arms directly to the side until your hands and elbows are just below shoulder height, exhaling. Lower slowly to the starting position, inhaling.

Muscles Used:
  Prime movers: deltoids
  Assistant movers: traps

START   FINISH

INCLINE PRESS

Starting Position: Sit on an incline bench with a barbell held at your chest and your hands slightly more than shoulder-width apart in a pronated grip. Your knees should be bent, with the feet comfortably apart and flat on the floor for stability.

Movement: Press the bar to arm's length directly above the shoulders, exhaling. Slowly lower the bar to the starting position, inhaling. Keep your back flat on the bench throughout the motion.

Muscles Used:

Prime movers: pecs and triceps

Assistant movers: deltoids

Variations:

- Use dumbbells instead of a barbell. You can alternate your arms or use both at the same time.

- Use a barbell or dumbbells in a standing position on a standing incline bench. To protect your back when using this position, be sure your knees are slightly bent and your back remains flat against the bench at all times.

START

FINISH

BENT-ARM PULLOVER

Starting Position: Lie supine on a bench with your feet flat on the floor. Hold a barbell on your chest with a pronated grip, hands about six inches apart.

Movement: Keeping your arms bent, swing the bar over your head and lower it slowly toward the floor while inhaling. Be careful not to go too far—stay within a comfortable range of motion. Return to the starting position, exhaling. Keep your head, back, and buttocks on the bench and your elbows approximately shoulder-width apart throughout the movement.

Precaution: This is a demanding exercise, which can put you in an arched-back position if done incorrectly. It should be considered an advanced exercise to be attempted only after you have been training for some time.

Muscles Used:
Prime movers: lats
Assistant movers: triceps and deltoids

Variations:

■ Use dumbbell(s) instead of a barbell.

■ Use a supinated grip. This works the triceps more.

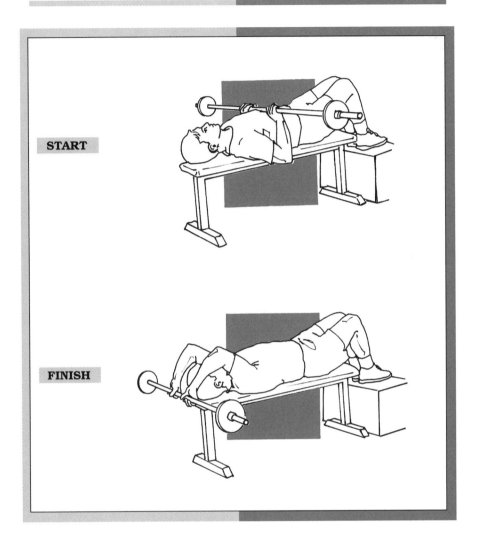

START

FINISH

PRONE SHOULDER ROW

Starting Position: Lying on a high bench, take a pronated grip on a barbell with the hands slightly more than shoulder-width apart.

Movement: Pull the bar to your chest while exhaling, keeping your elbows away from your body and above the bar. Return slowly to the starting position, inhaling.

Muscles Used:
Prime movers: lats, biceps, brachialis, and deltoids
Assistant movers: teres and rhomboids

Variation:
- Do the same movement standing, bent forward at the hips, with your upper body parallel to the floor, forehead supported on a high bench or table, and knees slightly bent.

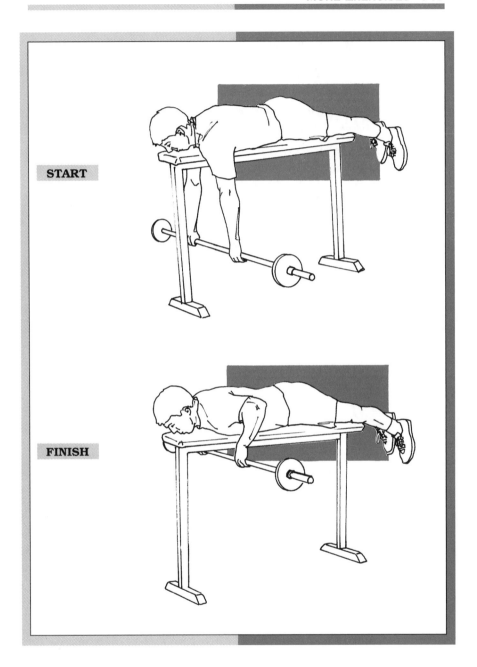

START

FINISH

SHOULDER SHRUG

Starting Position: Stand in front of the stack-weight bench press station with your back and arms straight. Hold the bar in a pronated grip with your hands shoulder-width apart and shoulders dropped forward and down.

Movement: Keeping your back and arms straight and looking straight ahead, pull the shoulders as high as possible, exhaling. Return slowly to the starting position, inhaling.

Muscles Used:
Prime movers: traps
Assistant movers: rhomboids and neck muscles

Variations:

- Pull the shoulders up and back or up and forward.

- Use a mixed (alternating) grip. This gives a more secure grasp on the bar. Reverse your grip each set.

- Use dumbbells instead of a barbell.

- Use the stack-weights low-pulley station.

START   FINISH

BENT-OVER ARM LATERAL RAISE

Starting Position: Sitting on the edge of a bench or low chair, lean forward until your torso is touching your thighs. With your hands directly below your shoulders, grasp dumbbells with the palms facing in and elbows slightly bent.

Movement: Keeping your elbows bent, raise your arms to the sides until your hands are at shoulder height while exhaling. Lower slowly to the starting position, inhaling.

Muscles Used:

Prime movers: deltoids, trapezius, and rhomboids

Variation:

- Do the same movement while lying prone on a high, flat bench.

START   FINISH

BENT-OVER TRICEPS PRESS

Starting Position: Stand, bent forward at the hips, with the upper body parallel to the floor and your weight supported on a bench or chair by your right arm. Grasp a dumbbell in your left hand, palm facing in, with your left elbow at your side, bent at 90°. Your knees should be slightly bent.

Movement: Keeping your left elbow close to your side, extend your lower arm behind until it is straight and horizontal while exhaling. Return slowly to the starting position, inhaling.

Muscles Used:
Prime movers: triceps
Assistant movers: deltoids and lats

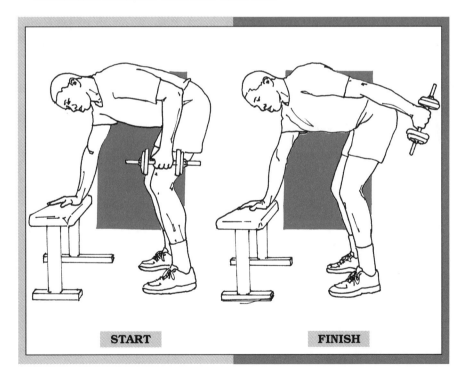

START   FINISH

CHINS

Starting Position: Take a pronated grip on a bar (or chin station on stack weights) with your hands shoulder-width apart. Hang from the bar with your arms straight, looking straight ahead, knees bent, and ankles crossed.

Movement: Pull up until your chin reaches the bar, exhaling. Lower slowly to the starting position, inhaling.

Muscles Used:
Prime movers: biceps, brachialis, and lats
Assistant movers: rhomboids
Stabilizers: pecs and teres

Variations:

■ Do partial chin-ups if the full motion is too difficult at first. That is, begin standing on a stool, bench, or chair so that your arms are partially bent, then proceed as described above.

■ Use a supinated grip. This works the wrist flexors more.

■ Do assisted or eccentric chins—step up to a chin position using a bench or chair. Lower yourself slowly, with control, to a hanging position. Repeat.

■ Vary the width of your grip.

START   FINISH

DIPS

Starting Position: Support your body on parallel/dip bars, with your arms straight, palms facing in, and back straight. Look straight ahead and hang free, with the knees bent and ankles crossed.

Movement: Lower your body by bending the elbows to approximately 90° while inhaling. Straighten your arms, returning to the starting position, exhaling. Use a controlled motion to avoid swinging.

Muscles Used:

Prime movers: triceps

Assistant movers: pecs, lats, and deltoids

Variations:

- Do partial dips, lowering yourself only part way down at first, if a 90° elbow bend is too difficult.

- Do assisted or eccentric dips—step up to the start position using a bench, stool, or chair. Lower yourself slowly, with control, until your elbows are bent at 90°. Repeat.

START   **FINISH**

WRIST FLEXION

Starting Position: Sit with a dumbbell in each hand, using a supinated grip. Lay your forearms on top of your thighs, with the crease of the wrists just in front of your knees.

Movement: With your palms facing up, flex the wrists, lifting the dumbbells toward you. Return to the start position. Keep your forearms flat on your legs throughout. Breathe evenly.

Muscles Used:

Prime movers: wrist flexors

Variation:

- This exercise can be done with a barbell, seated in front of a low-pulley station, or on a wrist and forearm machine. (Some machines have a wrist-flexion station.)

START   FINISH

WRIST EXTENSION

Starting Position: Sit with a dumbbell in each hand, using a pronated grip. Lay your forearms flat on top of your thighs, with the crease of your wrists just in front of your knees.

Movement: Keeping your palms facing down and away from you, extend the wrists, lifting the dumbbells toward you. Return to the start position. Keep your forearms flat on your legs throughout. Breathe evenly.

Muscles Used:

Prime movers: wrist extensors

Variation:

■ This exercise can be done with a barbell, seated in front of a low-pulley station, or on a wrist and forearm machine. (Some machines have a wrist-extension station.)

START   FINISH

WRIST ADDUCTION AND ABDUCTION

Starting Position: Standing, grasp a dumbbell in each hand, with your arms hanging at your sides, palms facing in.

Movement: Alternately bend your wrists up toward the front (thumb up) then up toward the back (little finger up). Keep your arms straight throughout and breathe evenly.

Muscles Used:

Prime movers: wrist extensors and flexors

Variation:

■ Wrist abduction and adduction can also be done using a small, straight handle and a low-/high-pulley, respectively.

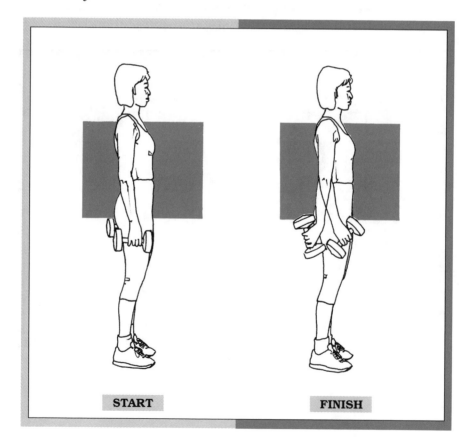

START   FINISH

Hand Grip

Starting Position: Hold a spring-grip or foam-grip hand exerciser, a racquetball, or a tennis ball.

Movement: Squeeze with the fingers and hand.

Muscles Used:
Prime movers: wrist and finger flexors

Variation:

■ Some stack-weight machines have a hand-grip station.

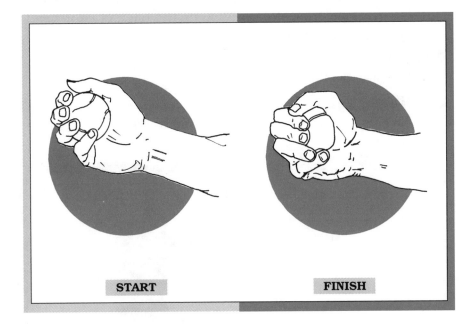

START   FINISH

REVERSE CURL-UP

Starting Position: Lie supine on the floor, with your arms on the floor at your sides, knees bent and together. Flex your hips so that your feet are off the floor and your lower back is pressed flat to the floor. (To get your legs in position, drag your heels along the floor as you pull your knees up toward your chest.)

Movement: Tighten your abdominals to pull your knees toward the shoulders (hips coming off the floor slightly), exhaling. Pause momentarily, then lower the hips slowly to the starting position, inhaling. Keep the back of your head on the floor throughout the movement.

Muscles Used:
Prime movers: abdominals

Variation:
- Place your hands behind your head to make the exercise more difficult.

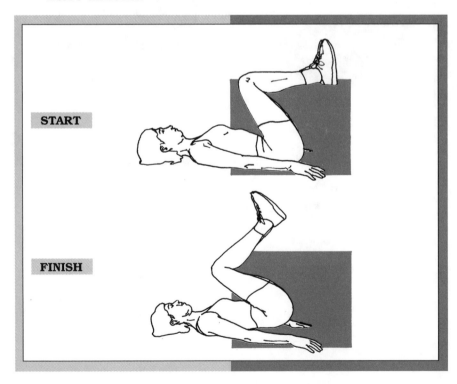

START

FINISH

SIDE BEND

Starting Position: Stand sideways to the stack weight's chest-press station, with your right side nearest the bar. Bend sideways to the right and grasp the bar with your right hand, palm facing your side. Keep the right arm straight and the left arm bent with the hand beside the head throughout the movement.

Movement: Bend laterally (not forward or back) to the left as far as you can comfortably, exhaling. Return to the upright (starting) position, inhaling. Repeat, then change sides.

Precautions: Keep the weight fairly light to minimize pressure on the spinal column. Keep your knees slightly bent.

Muscles Used:
Prime movers: paraspinals and obliques
Assistant movers: quads
Stabilizers: traps

Variation:
■ Use a dumbbell instead of the chest-press station.

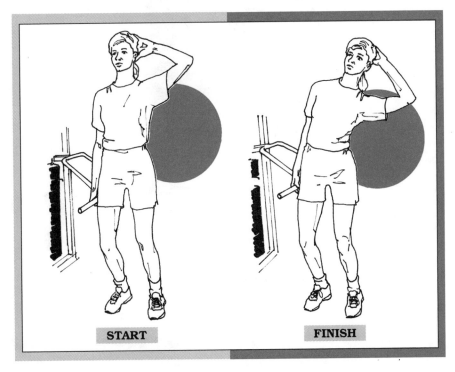

START   FINISH

SEATED SHOULDER ROW

Starting Position: Sit with your back flat against the chair's back and your feet flat on the floor. Hold your arms straight in front, hands a little below chest level, tubing lightly stretched and anchored in front at chest height.

Movement: Keeping your elbows close to your sides, pull your hands toward your trunk, inhaling. Return to starting position, exhaling.

Muscles Used:
Prime movers: biceps, traps, rhomboids, and deltoids
Assistant movers: teres and spinatus
Stabilizers: paraspinals

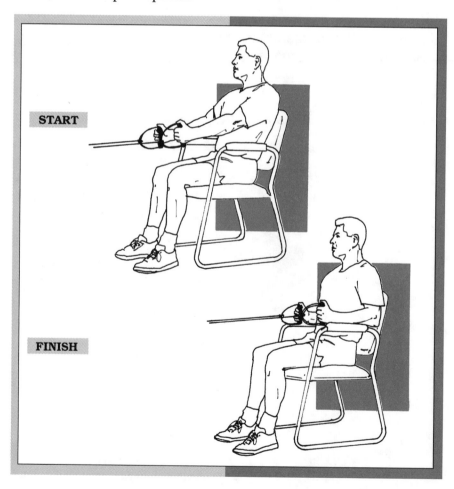

START

FINISH

SHOULDER ADDUCTION

Starting Position: Stand with your left side toward the stack weight's high-pulley station, a little more than an arm's length away from it. Grasp the pulley handle with your left hand, palm down, your elbow slightly bent, and your hand just below shoulder height.

Movement: Keeping your palm down, exhale as you pull your arm down to your side. Keep your shoulder down (not "hunched"). Return slowly to the start position, inhaling. Repeat, then change to the other arm.

Muscles Used:
Prime movers: pecs, lats, rhomboids, and teres major
Stabilizers: deltoids and traps

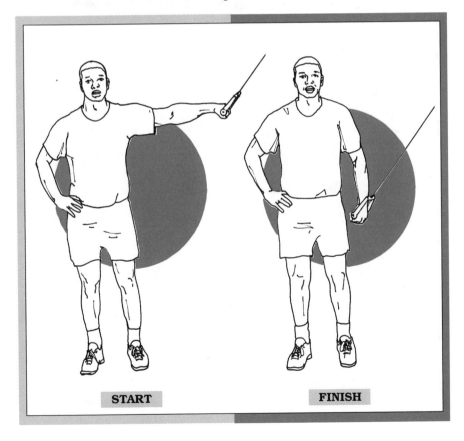

START   FINISH

SHOULDER EXTENSION

Starting Position: Stand facing the stack weight's high-pulley station, just over an arm's length away. Grasp the pulley handle with your palm down, your elbow slightly bent, and your hand just below shoulder height.

Movement: Keeping your palm down, exhale as you pull your arm down to your side. Keep your shoulder down. Return slowly to the start position, inhaling. Repeat, then change to the other arm.

Muscles Used:

Prime movers: lats, teres major, and traps

Stabilizers: pecs, deltoid, abdominals, and paraspinals

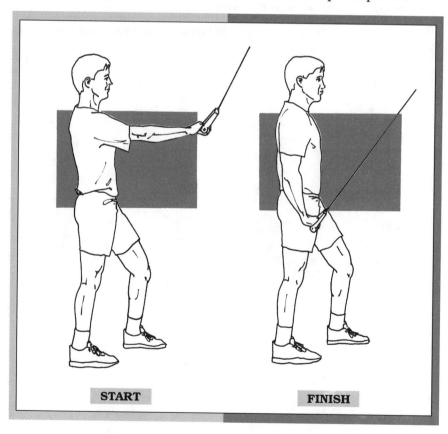

START   FINISH

Single Leg Press

Starting Position: Sit on a chair with the center of the tubing around one foot (a loop around the arch will help secure the tubing on your foot). Keep the opposite leg bent, with your foot flat on the floor. Start with your knee bent at 90° and anchor the tubing, lightly stretched with the hands at the chest.

Movement: Press your leg out until the knee is almost straight, exhaling. Return slowly to the start position, inhaling. Repeat, then change legs. (You can double the tubing for more resistance.)

Muscles Used:
Prime movers: quads, gluts, and hamstrings
Stabilizers: paraspinals, hip adductors, and abductors

Variation:

- This exercise can also be done lying supine on the floor, using the same movement as described above.

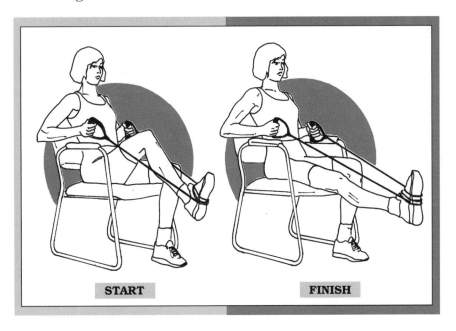

START   FINISH

SHIN PULL

Starting Position: Sit on the floor, a chair, or a bench facing the stack weight's low-pulley station. Hook the handle of the pulley over the toe of your right shoe. Sit with your right leg straight, the toe pointed up, and the ankle plantar flexed (pointing slightly toward the pulley station). Keep your left leg bent and place your foot flat on the floor.

Movement: Keeping your right knee straight, dorsiflex the ankle (pull the toe toward you). Lower slowly to the start position. Repeat. Breathe evenly. Repeat with the other leg.

Muscles Used:
Prime movers: tibialis anterior
Assistant movers: peroneus
Stabilizers: quads

Variations:

■ This exercise can be done without equipment. (See Shin Pull in Chapter 6, page 74.)

■ You can also do this exercise with tubing. Anchor the tubing in front of you, make a loop around your foot, and use the same movement as described above.

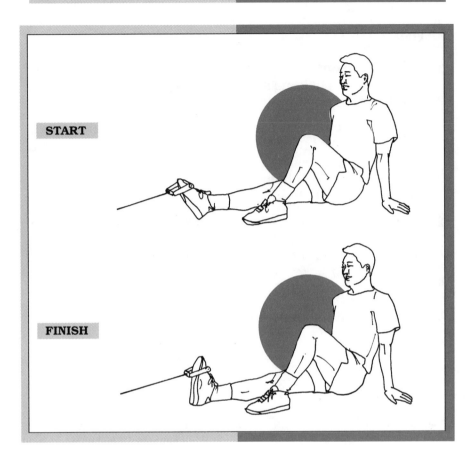

START

FINISH

LUNGE

Starting Position: Stand with your back straight and look straight ahead, holding a dumbbell in each hand, with your arms hanging at your sides.

Movement: Step forward with the right foot, lowering your body. Your right knee should be over your right foot as you lower your left knee toward the floor, exhaling. Return to the starting position, inhaling. Repeat with the left leg going forward. Alternate legs.

Precautions: The heel of the rear foot should come off the floor as you lunge forward. When in the low position, the knee of your front leg should be just over your foot.

Muscles Used:
Prime movers: quads and gluts
Stabilizers: paraspinals, abdominals, and the muscles of the arms and shoulders

Variations:

- Use a barbell held on your shoulders and secured with a pronated grip.

- Start with no external resistance for a gentle beginning.

START   FINISH

STANDING CALF RAISE

Starting Position: Stand with your toes on the center of the tubing and your feet shoulder-width apart. Hold the lightly stretched tubing in each hand with your arms at your sides.

Movement: Keep your legs straight and exhale as you raise up on your toes as far as you can. Lower slowly to the start position, inhaling.

Muscles Used:
Prime movers: gastrocs and soleii
Assistant movers: peroneus

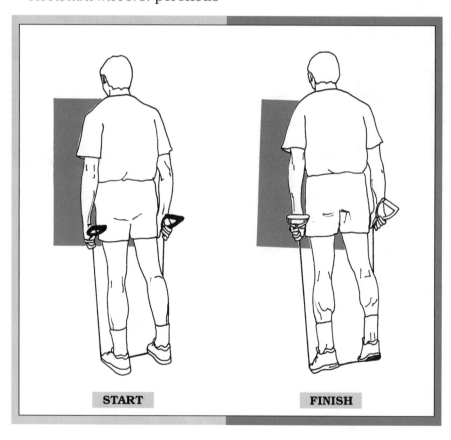

START   FINISH

CLEAN

Starting Position: Bend down to grasp a barbell, with your feet shoulder-width apart, knees bent at 90°, back straight, and looking straight ahead. Your arms should be straight, your hands in a pronated grip and slightly more than shoulder-width apart.

Movement: With a smooth movement, return to a standing position, lifting the barbell to shoulder height, your elbows below and in front of the bar. Lift primarily with the legs (arms remaining straight) to initiate the movement. Start to pull with the arms and shoulders as the bar passes the knees. Exhale as you lift the weight; inhale as you return it to the floor.

Muscles Used:
Prime movers: quads, gluts, traps, deltoids, and paraspinals
Assistant movers: lats, rhomboids, biceps, brachialis, and hamstrings

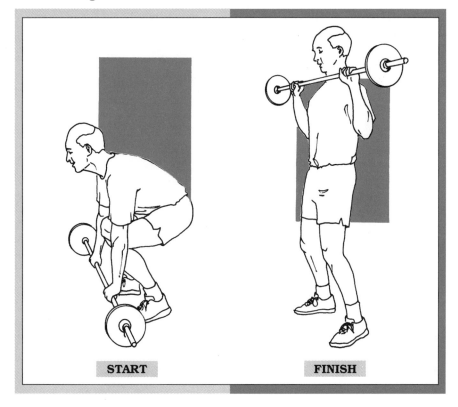

START FINISH

BENCH STEP-UP

Starting Position: Stand in front of a sturdy bench 6 to 12 inches (15 to 30 cm) high to allow a maximum knee bend of 90°. Keep your back straight, look straight ahead, and hold a dumbbell in each hand, with your arms hanging at your sides.

Movement: Step up onto the bench, leading with the right leg. Pause momentarily when both feet are on the bench. Step down smoothly from the bench, leading with the right leg again. Perform half of your reps leading with the right leg, half leading with the left. Exhale as you step up; inhale as you step down.

Muscles Used:
Prime movers: quads and gluts
Assistant movers: hamstrings, hip flexors, gastrocs, and tensor fascia latae

Variations:

- Use a barbell held on your shoulders and secured with a pronated grip.

- Start with no external resistance for a gentle beginning.

START   FINISH

10

TRAINING
FOR YOUR
FAVORITE
SPORT

The RT routines in Chapters 6, 7, and 8 provide overall, balanced development and a firm foundation of muscular endurance. They are great starter routines and perfect programs for general health and fitness.

But if you have a favorite sport or recreational activity, you may want to go beyond these programs and follow a training routine that is sport specific. You can do this by emphasizing exercises that strengthen the muscles most important in your sport and by changing the focus to power or strength development if your sport demands it. So whether you're an athlete training for a competitive sport or you just want to play a more wicked game of weekend tennis, RT can help improve your performance.

Recognizing that everyone is different, we've approached sport-specific training in two ways. The first approach, outlined in the section called "Creating Your Own Program," is for those who would like to play a part in devising their own routine. It allows you to utilize your knowledge of the sport—and of your own strengths and weaknesses—to choose the exercises, training format, and training variables that will work best for you. The second approach, covered in the section called "RT Recipes: A to Z," is for those who want to train for their sport by following step-by-step directions. This section includes structured routines for a wide variety of sports.

As a general rule, we recommend that if you're just getting into RT you do the tubing routine in Chapter 7 or one of the core routines in Chapter 8 for at least 12 weeks before pursuing a sport-specific routine.

CREATING YOUR OWN PROGRAM

With the help of Chart 10.1 on page 171, you can design your own routine for any of the sports listed. With a little more patience and ingenuity, you can do the same for virtually every sport. Sports are listed in the left-hand column; the physical requirements and the most important muscles are noted in the other two columns.

To design your program:

■ Start with your current routine (from Chapter 7 or 8) and add exercises to it or replace current exercises with others that are more specific to the demands of your sport. To do this, match up the muscles listed in the "Most Important Muscles" column in the chart with the "Muscles Used" at the end of each exercise description in Chapters 6 to 9. This will help you determine the most important exercises. You can draw on any of the exercises in these four chapters to devise your own routine.

■ Include 10 to (a maximum of) 15 exercises in your routine. You'll be at or near the top end of this range if muscular

Chart 10.1 Sport-Specific Training		
Activity	Requirements (power or muscular endurance)[1]	Most important muscles[2]
Alpine skiing	Power and muscular endurance	Quads, gluts, gastrocs, and soleus
Baseball	Power	Deltoids, wrist flexors and extensors, teres, paraspinals, lats, and obliques
Basketball	Power and muscular endurance	Quads, gluts, gastrocs, and soleus
Bicycling	Muscular endurance and power	Quads, gluts, gastrocs, and soleus
Cross-country skiing	Muscular endurance	Hamstrings, gastrocs, soleus, and hip flexors
Field hockey	Muscular endurance and power	Quads, gluts, tensor fascia latae, hip adductors, obliques, deltoids, wrist flexors, and wrist extensors
Figure skating	Muscular endurance and power	Quads, gluts, tensor fascia latae, hip adductors, and obliques
Football	Power and muscular endurance	Quads, gluts, obliques, deltoids, and traps
Golf	Power	Deltoids, wrist flexors and extensors, teres, paraspinals, lats, and obliques
Handball	Muscular endurance	Wrist flexors, wrist extensors, deltoids, pecs, lats, hip adductors, gluts, and tensor fascia latae
Ice hockey	Muscular endurance and power	Quads, gluts, tensor fascia latae, hip adductors, obliques, deltoids, wrist flexors, and wrist extensors
Paddling/rowing (canoeing, kayaking, rowing)	Muscular endurance and power	Obliques, deltoids, triceps, biceps, paraspinals, quads, hip flexors, lats, and teres

Chart 10.1 Sport-Specific Training (continued)		
Activity	**Requirements (power or muscular endurance)[1]**	**Most important muscles[2]**
Racquet sports (badminton, squash, racquetball, tennis)	Muscular endurance	Wrist flexors, wrist extensors, deltoids, pecs, lats, hip adductors, gluts, and tensor fascia latae
Rugby	Power and muscular endurance	Quads, gluts, obliques, deltoids, and traps
Running	Muscular endurance	Hamstrings, gastrocs, soleus, and hip flexors
Soccer	Muscular endurance and power	Quads, gluts, tensor fascia latae, hip adductors, obliques, deltoids, wrist flexors, and wrist extensors
Speed skating	Power and muscular endurance	Quads, gluts, gastrocs, soleus, hip adductors, and tensor fascia latae
Swimming	Muscular endurance	Deltoids, pecs, lats, triceps and traps
Volleyball	Power and muscular endurance	Quads, gluts, gastrocs, and soleus

[1]Although an activity calls for a "power" program, note that not all exercises lend themselves to a power (low rep., high weight) approach. The curl-up is a good example. This exercise should be made more demanding by increasing the sets and reps, not the weight. Sets of 40 and 50 curl-ups are not uncommon for highly fit individuals. Just be sure to work up to the high repetitions gradually.

[2]The abdominals and paraspinals play important stabilizing and supportive roles in all activities. Hence, exercises for these muscles should be included in all programs. (These muscles are only noted here for activities in which they play a primary role.)

performance is a dominant characteristic of your sport *and* you're prepared to devote a little more time to RT. Make sure you put your exercises in an order that follows the work-rest principle as outlined in Chapter 4. You may want to split the exercises into two, three, or more minicircuits to keep your routine as quick and convenient as possible.

■ Determine the number of repetitions and sets you should do (as shown in Chart 4.2 on page 44). For some of the activities in our sport-specific training chart, both power and muscular endurance are noted. While it may over-simplify things, we can generally say that for competition, shorter distances, and stop-and-start activities, power should be emphasized; for recreation, longer distances, and sustained activities, muscular endurance should be the focus.

■ If your chosen sport is not listed in the chart, first analyze the demands and movements of the sport to determine the most important muscles, then work through the process in the three points above.

RT RECIPES: A TO Z

Well, almost A to Z. Sixteen recipes are included here—from 'A' for alpine skiing to 'W' for wrestling. Some routines are suitable for more than one sport because the demands of the sports are so similar. Racquet sports are grouped together for this reason. So are canoeing, kayaking, and rowing (under the heading Paddling/Rowing.)

Exercises are included from the four routines in Chapters 6 to 8 and the catalogue in Chapter 9 (including some that appeared as variations). Page number references are provided for each exercise. If you don't have access to the equipment required for a particular exercise, substitute the equivalent exercise from one of the other routines. (Let the muscle groups listed and the joint action be your guide in choosing an alternate exercise when necessary.)

For each program:

- The primary goal—development of strength or power or muscular endurance—is noted. If there is some overlap in what the sport requires, a secondary emphasis is noted in brackets.

- The program variables—sets, reps, resistance, and rest period—relate to the primary goal. An (S) for strength, (P) for power, or (M.E.) for muscular endurance is placed beside any exercise where the *repetitions* or *resistance* should differ from those noted in the program variables. Refer to the footnote for that program to confirm the proper reps/resistance.

- For proper order, do the exercises in the left-hand column of the list, followed by those in the right-hand column.

Running, soccer, and swimming each require a combination of power and muscular endurance. Because muscular endurance is improved nicely by the activity itself, the focus of the RT program for these sports is on developing power to take advantage of the special benefits available when working with resistance equipment.

The programs follow.

ALPINE SKIING

Goal: Power (and Muscular Endurance)

Program Variables: three to four sets, five to eight reps or more, moderate to high resistance, and short to moderate rest periods.

Exercise List:

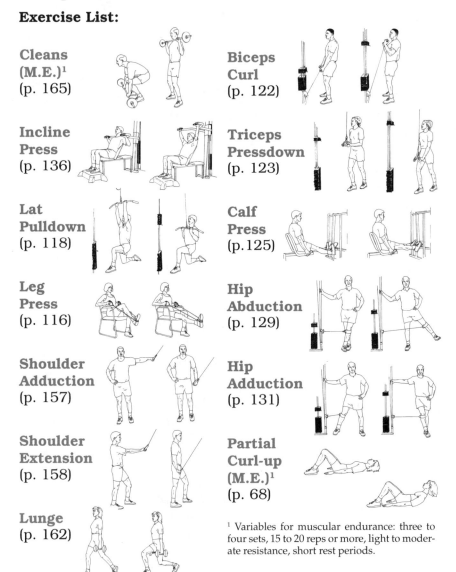

Cleans
(M.E.)[1]
(p. 165)

Biceps
Curl
(p. 122)

Incline
Press
(p. 136)

Triceps
Pressdown
(p. 123)

Lat
Pulldown
(p. 118)

Calf
Press
(p.125)

Leg
Press
(p. 116)

Hip
Abduction
(p. 129)

Shoulder
Adduction
(p. 157)

Hip
Adduction
(p. 131)

Shoulder
Extension
(p. 158)

Partial
Curl-up
(M.E.)[1]
(p. 68)

Lunge
(p. 162)

[1] Variables for muscular endurance: three to four sets, 15 to 20 reps or more, light to moderate resistance, short rest periods.

BASEBALL

Goal: Power

Program Variables: three to four sets, five to eight reps, moderate to heavy resistance, and moderate rest periods.

Exercise List:

Cleans
(M.E.)[1]
(p. 165)

Chest
Press
(p. 99)

Bent-Arm
Pullover
(p. 138)

Leg
Press
(p. 159)

Upright
Row
(p. 111)

Triceps
Press
(p. 107)

Biceps
Curl
(p. 122)

Partial
Curl-up
(M.E.)[1]
(p. 68)

Hip
Abduction
(p. 129)

Hip
Adduction
(p. 131)

Shoulder
Extension
(p. 158)

Shoulder
Adduction
(p. 157)

Wrist
Flexion
(p. 150)

Wrist
Extension
(p. 151)

Wrist
Adduction/
Abduction
(p. 152)

[1] Variables for muscular endurance: three to four sets, 15 to 20 reps or more, light to moderate resistance, and short rest periods.

BASKETBALL

Goal: Power (and Muscular Endurance)

Program Variables: three to four sets, five to eight reps, moderate resistance, and short rest periods.

Exercise List:

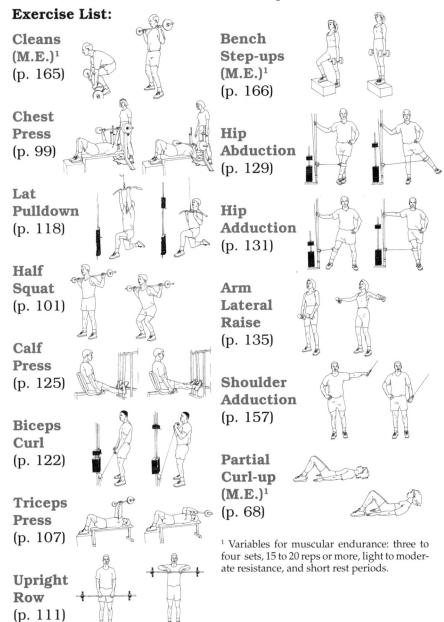

Cleans
(M.E.)[1]
(p. 165)

Chest
Press
(p. 99)

Lat
Pulldown
(p. 118)

Half
Squat
(p. 101)

Calf
Press
(p. 125)

Biceps
Curl
(p. 122)

Triceps
Press
(p. 107)

Upright
Row
(p. 111)

Bench
Step-ups
(M.E.)[1]
(p. 166)

Hip
Abduction
(p. 129)

Hip
Adduction
(p. 131)

Arm
Lateral
Raise
(p. 135)

Shoulder
Adduction
(p. 157)

Partial
Curl-up
(M.E.)[1]
(p. 68)

[1] Variables for muscular endurance: three to four sets, 15 to 20 reps or more, light to moderate resistance, and short rest periods.

CROSS-COUNTRY SKIING

Goal: Muscular Endurance

Program Variables: three to four sets, 15 to 20 reps or more, moderate resistance, and short rest periods.

Exercise List:

Leg
Press
(p. 116)

Chest
Press
(p. 99)

Lat
Pulldown
(p. 118)

Calf
Press
(p. 125)

Upright
Row
(p. 111)

Triceps
Pressdown
(p. 123)

Shoulder
Extension
(p. 158)

Seated
Shoulder
Row
(p. 127)

Partial
Curl-up
(p. 68)

Wrist
Flexion
(p. 150)

Wrist
Extension
(p. 151)

Wrist
Adduction/
Abduction
(p. 152)

CYCLING

Goal: Muscular Endurance (and Power)

Program Variables: three to four sets, 15 to 20 reps or more, moderate resistance, and short rest periods.

Exercise List:

Cleans
(P)[1]
(p. 165)

Chest
Press
(p. 99)

Seated
Shoulder
Row
(p. 127)

Leg
Press (P)[1]
(p. 116)

Calf
Press (P)[1]
(p. 125)

Biceps
Curl
(p. 122)

Upright
Row
(p. 111)

Triceps
Pressdown
(p. 123)

Lat
Pulldown
(p. 118)

Bench
Step-ups
(p. 166)

Partial
Curl-up
(p. 68)

Shin
Pull
(p. 160)

[1] Variables for power: three to four sets, five to eight reps, moderate resistance, and short rest periods.

FOOTBALL

Goal: Strength (and Power)

Program Variables: three to four sets, one to four reps, moderate to heavy resistance, and moderate to long rest periods.

Exercise List:

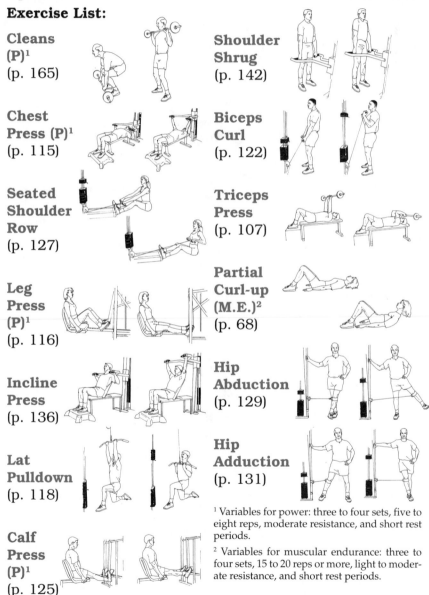

Cleans
(P)[1]
(p. 165)

Shoulder
Shrug
(p. 142)

Chest
Press (P)[1]
(p. 115)

Biceps
Curl
(p. 122)

Seated
Shoulder
Row
(p. 127)

Triceps
Press
(p. 107)

Leg
Press
(P)[1]
(p. 116)

Partial
Curl-up
(M.E.)[2]
(p. 68)

Incline
Press
(p. 136)

Hip
Abduction
(p. 129)

Lat
Pulldown
(p. 118)

Hip
Adduction
(p. 131)

Calf
Press
(P)[1]
(p. 125)

[1] Variables for power: three to four sets, five to eight reps, moderate resistance, and short rest periods.

[2] Variables for muscular endurance: three to four sets, 15 to 20 reps or more, light to moderate resistance, and short rest periods.

ICE HOCKEY

Goal: Power (and Muscular Endurance)

Program Variables: three to four sets, five to eight reps, moderate to heavy resistance, and short rest periods.

Exercise List:

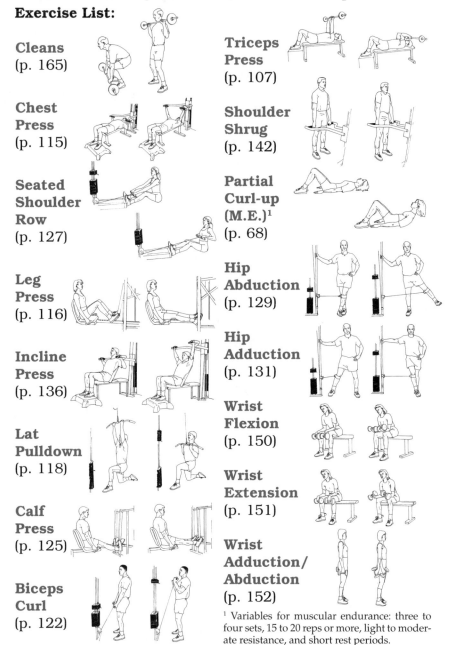

Cleans (p. 165)

Chest Press (p. 115)

Seated Shoulder Row (p. 127)

Leg Press (p. 116)

Incline Press (p. 136)

Lat Pulldown (p. 118)

Calf Press (p. 125)

Biceps Curl (p. 122)

Triceps Press (p. 107)

Shoulder Shrug (p. 142)

Partial Curl-up (M.E.)[1] (p. 68)

Hip Abduction (p. 129)

Hip Adduction (p. 131)

Wrist Flexion (p. 150)

Wrist Extension (p. 151)

Wrist Adduction/ Abduction (p. 152)

[1] Variables for muscular endurance: three to four sets, 15 to 20 reps or more, light to moderate resistance, and short rest periods.

IN-LINE ROLLER SKATING

Goal: Muscular Endurance

Program Variables: three to four sets, 15 to 20 reps or more, light to moderate resistance, and short rest periods.

Exercise List:

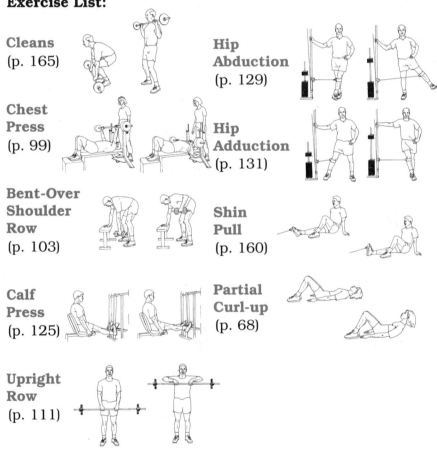

Cleans
(p. 165)

Chest Press
(p. 99)

Bent-Over Shoulder Row
(p. 103)

Calf Press
(p. 125)

Upright Row
(p. 111)

Hip Abduction
(p. 129)

Hip Adduction
(p. 131)

Shin Pull
(p. 160)

Partial Curl-up
(p. 68)

PADDLING/ROWING

Goal: Power (and Muscular Endurance)

Program Variables: three to four sets, five to eight reps or more, light to moderate resistance, and short rest periods.

Exercise List:

Cleans
(p. 165)

Upright Row
(p. 111)

Triceps Pressdown
(p. 123)

Lat Pulldown
(p. 118)

Chest Press
(p. 99)

Calf Press (M.E.)[1]
(p. 125)

Seated Shoulder Row
(p. 127)

Shin Pull (M.E)[1]
(p. 160)

Leg Press
(p. 116)

Partial Curl-up
(p. 68)

Biceps Curl (Pronated Grip)
(p. 122)

[1] Variables for muscular endurance: three to four sets, 15 to 20 reps, light to moderate resistance, and short rest periods.

Shoulder Shrug
(p. 142)

RACQUET SPORTS

Goal: Strength (and Muscular Endurance)

Program Variables: three to four sets, five to eight reps or more, light to moderate resistance, and short rest periods.

Exercise List:

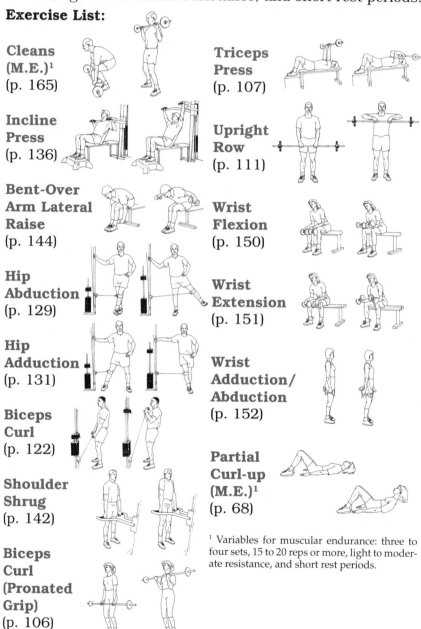

Cleans
(M.E.)[1]
(p. 165)

Incline
Press
(p. 136)

Bent-Over
Arm Lateral
Raise
(p. 144)

Hip
Abduction
(p. 129)

Hip
Adduction
(p. 131)

Biceps
Curl
(p. 122)

Shoulder
Shrug
(p. 142)

Biceps
Curl
(Pronated
Grip)
(p. 106)

Triceps
Press
(p. 107)

Upright
Row
(p. 111)

Wrist
Flexion
(p. 150)

Wrist
Extension
(p. 151)

Wrist
Adduction/
Abduction
(p. 152)

Partial
Curl-up
(M.E.)[1]
(p. 68)

[1] Variables for muscular endurance: three to four sets, 15 to 20 reps or more, light to moderate resistance, and short rest periods.

RUGBY

Goal: Power (and Strength)

Program Variables: three to four sets, five to eight reps, moderate to heavy resistance, and moderate rest periods.

Exercise List:

Cleans (M.E.)[1] (p. 165)

Chest Press (p. 115)

Seated Shoulder Row (p. 127)

Incline Press (p. 136)

Lat Pulldown (p. 118)

Leg Press (p. 116)

Biceps Curl (S)[2] (p. 122)

Triceps Pressdown (S)[2] (p. 123)

Calf Press (p. 125)

Hip Abduction (p. 129)

Hip Adduction (p. 131)

Partial Curl-up (M.E.)[1] (p. 68)

[1] Variables for muscular endurance: three to four sets, 15 to 20 reps, light to moderate resistance, and short rest periods.

[2] Variables for strength: three to four sets, one to four reps, moderate to heavy resistance, and moderate to long rest periods.

RUNNING (DISTANCE)

Goal: Muscular Endurance

Program Variables: three to four sets, 15 to 20 reps or more, light to moderate resistance, and short rest periods.

Exercise List:

Cleans
(p. 165)

Chest Press
(p. 115)

Bent-Over One-Arm Row
(p. 86)

Leg Press
(p. 116)

Upright Row
(p. 111)

Triceps Pressdown
(p. 123)

Calf Press
(p. 125)

Shin Pull
(p. 160)

Partial Curl-up
(p. 68)

SOCCER

Goal: Power (and Muscular Endurance)

Program Variables: three to four sets, five to eight reps or more, moderate to heavy resistance, and short to moderate rest periods.

Exercise List:

Cleans
(M.E.)[1]
(p. 165)

Calf
Press
(p. 125)

Incline
Press
(p. 136)

Hip
Abduction
(p. 129)

Bent-Arm
Pullover
(p. 138)

Hip
Adduction
(p. 131)

Leg
Press
(p. 116)

Partial
Curl-up
(M.E.)[1]
(p. 68)

Biceps
Curl
(p. 106)

Shin
Pull
(M.E.)[1]
(p. 160)

Triceps
Press
(p. 107)

[1] Variables for muscular endurance: three to four sets, 15 to 20 reps, light to moderate resistance, and short rest periods.

Arm
Lateral
Raise
(p. 135)

SWIMMING

Goal: Power (and Muscular Endurance)

Program Variables: three to four sets, five to eight reps or more, light to moderate resistance, and short rest periods.

Exercise List:

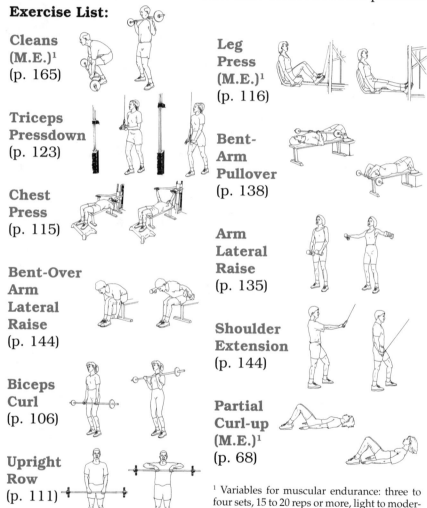

Cleans (M.E.)[1] (p. 165)

Triceps Pressdown (p. 123)

Chest Press (p. 115)

Bent-Over Arm Lateral Raise (p. 144)

Biceps Curl (p. 106)

Upright Row (p. 111)

Leg Press (M.E.)[1] (p. 116)

Bent-Arm Pullover (p. 138)

Arm Lateral Raise (p. 135)

Shoulder Extension (p. 144)

Partial Curl-up (M.E.)[1] (p. 68)

[1] Variables for muscular endurance: three to four sets, 15 to 20 reps or more, light to moderate resistance, and short rest periods.

VOLLEYBALL

Goal: Power (and Muscular Endurance)

Program Variables: three to four sets, five to eight reps, moderate resistance, and short rest periods.

Exercise List:

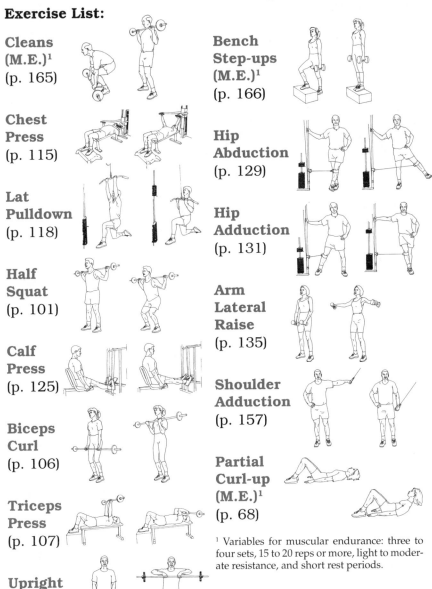

Cleans (M.E.)[1] (p. 165)

Chest Press (p. 115)

Lat Pulldown (p. 118)

Half Squat (p. 101)

Calf Press (p. 125)

Biceps Curl (p. 106)

Triceps Press (p. 107)

Upright Row (p. 111)

Bench Step-ups (M.E.)[1] (p. 166)

Hip Abduction (p. 129)

Hip Adduction (p. 131)

Arm Lateral Raise (p. 135)

Shoulder Adduction (p. 157)

Partial Curl-up (M.E.)[1] (p. 68)

[1] Variables for muscular endurance: three to four sets, 15 to 20 reps or more, light to moderate resistance, and short rest periods.

WRESTLING

Goal: Strength (and Power)

Program Variables: three to four sets, one to four reps, moderate to high resistance, and moderate to long rest periods.

Exercise List:

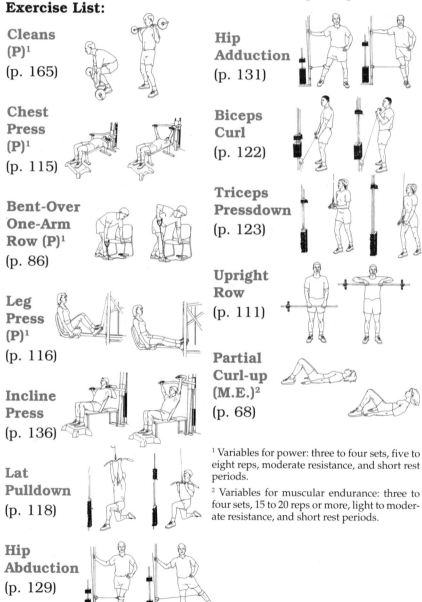

Cleans
(P)[1]
(p. 165)

Chest
Press
(P)[1]
(p. 115)

Bent-Over
One-Arm
Row (P)[1]
(p. 86)

Leg
Press
(P)[1]
(p. 116)

Incline
Press
(p. 136)

Lat
Pulldown
(p. 118)

Hip
Abduction
(p. 129)

Hip
Adduction
(p. 131)

Biceps
Curl
(p. 122)

Triceps
Pressdown
(p. 123)

Upright
Row
(p. 111)

Partial
Curl-up
(M.E.)[2]
(p. 68)

[1] Variables for power: three to four sets, five to eight reps, moderate resistance, and short rest periods.

[2] Variables for muscular endurance: three to four sets, 15 to 20 reps or more, light to moderate resistance, and short rest periods.

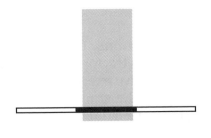

YOUR PERSONAL TRAINING RECORD

Refer to the example on the next page as you read the following explanation of how the chart works.

Exercises: Record the exercises in order down the second column. If there are any groupings (i.e., minicircuits) or a sequence other than the order in which the exercises are listed, you can indicate this in the first column. For example, if you're doing a routine of nine exercises divided into three minicircuits of three exercises each, write '1' in the Seq column beside the first three exercises as a reminder that this is your first minicircuit, a '2' beside the next three, and a '3' beside the final three. Note your sets and reps range in the Goal column.

Resistance Progression: Record your starting resistance in the first column under Resistance Progression. Record your new, heavier resistance in the next column each time you progress. You should also indicate the date that you increased for that particular exercise. You might simply circle the reps and sets on the day that you moved to this new, higher resistance.

Date, Sets, and Repetitions: Use a new column for *each* workout, noting the date in the top row and recording the sets and reps for each successive exercise in the rows below.

In the example shown, the starting weight for chest press was 50 pounds. Chris started out with two sets of 10 reps and progressed to two sets of 15 reps. On January 16th, Chris went to three sets, dropped the reps back to 10, and gradually increased the reps up to 15 again. On January 30th, Chris increased the weight to 60 pounds and dropped the reps back to 10 again.

Copy the Form: A blank personal training record is included following the example on the next page. We recommend that you make photocopies and use them as your training guide. Keeping track of your workouts helps you stay organized and on track. Your training record can be a great source of satisfaction and motivation as your workouts improve. Also, it is easier to make changes and improve your program if you know exactly what you have been doing.

PERSONAL TRAINING RECORD

Name: _CHRIS_

Program Start Date: _JAN. 5_   Review Date _FEB. 15_

Seq	Exercises	Goal Sets/Reps	Resistance Progression	Date, Sets and Repetitions (record each session)										
				1/5	1/7	1/9	1/12	1/14	1/16	1/19	1/21	1/23	1/26	1/28	1/30
	CHEST PRESS	3 / 10-15	50 60	2X 10	2X 12	2X 14	2X 15	3X 10	3X 12	3X 12	3X 14	3X 15	3X 10		

193

PERSONAL TRAINING RECORD

Name: _____

Program Start Date: _____   Review Date: _____

Seq	Exercises	Goal Sets/Reps	Resistance Progression	Date, Sets and Repetitions (record each session)

RECOMMENDED RESOURCES

HUMAN KINETICS RT TITLES

You may contact Human Kinetics Publishers, Inc. at 1-800-747-4457 or 1-800-465-7301 (Canada) to obtain their current catalog, which contains a complete list of their RT resources. Popular books include:

Strength Training for Women, by James Peterson, Cedric Bryant, and Susan Peterson.

Strength Training for Young Athletes, by William Kraemer and Steven Fleck.

Weight Training: Steps to Success, by Thomas Baechle and Barney Groves.

OTHER RT RESOURCES

Contact the publishers directly for cost and ordering information on the following titles.

The Complete Guide to Medicine Ball Training, by Vern Gambetta and Steve Odgers, Gambetta Sports Training Systems, P.O. Box 10277, Sarasota, FL 34278. Tel: (941) 378-1778 [In the U.S. 1-800-671-4045]. Fax: (941) 379-6310.

The Joy of Flex: A Thinking Man and Woman's Guide to Basic Bodybuilding, by Gareth Llewellyn and Greg Poole, Department of Physical Recreation and Athletics, Carleton University, 1125 Colonel By Drive, Ottawa, Ontario, Canada K1S 5B6. Tel: (613) 788-4480. Fax: (613) 788-4466.

Tubing: A New Way to a Great Shape! by Sandy Houston and Phil Campagna, Renova Physiotherapy Centre, #307-1597 Bedford Highway, Bedford, Nova Scotia, Canada B4A 1E7. Tel: (902) 835-6561. Fax: (902) 835-6562.

NUTRITION

These resources provide straightforward, sensible advice.

Canada's Food Guide to Healthy Eating. Health Canada pamphlet available free in Canada from public health units or departments.

Nancy Clark's Sports Nutrition Guidebook. Paperback book available from Human Kinetics Publishers.

The Food Guide Pyramid. Pamphlet available from U.S. Department of Agriculture, Human Nutrition Information Service, 6505 Belcrest Road, Hyattsville, MD 20782.

INDEX

ABOUT THE AUTHORS

Coauthors Brian Cook and Gordon Stewart combine more than 40 years' experience in the health and fitness field. They have taught athletes, instructors, and participants the theory and techniques of resistance training and designed countless individualized programs. They also are the coauthors of *Get Strong: A Sensible Guide to Strength Training for Fitness.*

Brian Cook has a bachelor of science degree in human performance. He has extensive experience coordinating employee fitness programs and developing and managing private fitness clubs in British Columbia, Ontario, and in Singapore. As a consultant, Cook has  trained staff in the fields of fitness, sport training, and rehabilitation. He is the senior kinesiologist at a large and progressive physiotherapy and rehabilitation clinic.

Cook has competed in a variety of sports, from track and field to flatwater canoe racing. An avid cyclist who lives in Burlington, Ontario, he enjoys a regular resistance-training program, and has returned to canoeing as a masters paddler.

Gordon Stewart has a master of science degree in kinesiology and more than 20 years' experience in fitness program management and consulting. Stewart specializes in health communications, serving a wide range of clients from his home base in Victoria, British Columbia. He is the author  of several books, including *Active Living: The Miracle Medicine for a Long and Healthy Life* and *Every Body's Fitness Book*.

A former decathlete, Stewart competed internationally for Canada in the 1970s. Along with resistance training, Stewart enjoys rowing and running to stay fit.